WOMEN:
TO PREACH◇
◇OR NOT
TO PREACH◇

◆
**21
Outstanding
Black Preachers
Say Yes!**
◆

WOMEN: TO PREACH OR NOT TO PREACH

21 Outstanding Black Preachers Say YES!

Edited by
ELLA PEARSON MITCHELL

JUDSON PRESS ®   **VALLEY FORGE**

The sermon by James A Forbes, Jr., first appeared in *Union Seminary Quarterly Review,* Volume 42, Number 4, 1988, and is used by permission.

The sermon "E.R.A.," by G. Daniel Jones, first appeared in *WATCHword,* volume 9, number 1 (September 1985).

Unless otherwise indicated, Bible quotations in this volume are from the Revised Standard Version of the Bible, copyrighted 1946, 1952 © 1971, 1973 by the Division of Christian Education of the National Council of the Churches of Christ in the U.S.A., and used by permission.

Other quotations of the Bible are from

Good News Bible, the Bible in Today's English Version. Copyright © American Bible Society 1966, 1971, 1976.

HOLY BIBLE New International Version, copyright © 1978, New York International Bible Society. Used by permission.

The Bible: A New Translation by James Moffatt. Copyright 1954 by James Moffatt. Reprinted by permission of Harper & Row, Publishers, Inc.

The Holy Bible, King James Version.

Library of Congress Cataloging-in-Publication Data

Women: to preach or not to preach?: 21 outstanding Black preachers say yes! / edited by Ella Pearson Mitchell.
    p. cm.
    ISBN 0-8170-1169-2
    1. Ordination of women—Christianity—Sermons. 2. Women clergy—United States—Sermons. 3. Sermons, American—Afro-American authors. I. Mitchell, Ella Pearson.
BV676.W585 1991
262'.14—dc20   91-12710
                                                      CIP

To the dim but cherished memory
of the untold hosts of women
whose call from God to the
ordained ministry was denied for generations
by their own sisters and brothers.

CONTENTS

PREFACE

The question of whether or not women should preach has already been answered abundantly in my life and writings, but there is much still unsaid as to why. Indeed, the answers are being increased day by day, and the witnesses to that answer are increasing in number and strength. It is time once again to record and share selections from the preached testimony, including this time not only the word of gifted sister preachers, (as was the case in the two volumes of *Those Preaching Women*), but enlisting the word of respected brothers as well. It is time also for that word to deal with this question directly, rather than simply to have persons preach and let the power of their word suggest an answer. This book meets the question of female preachers head-on.

The authors included are persons known to share my position and to be highly articulate. Some are better known to me than to many of my readers, but all will introduce themselves with their biblical soundness and forceful logic. Meanwhile, the introduction will present a historical survey of the positions on the question which have arisen through the centuries, both in secular thought and in the Hebrew-Christian tradition, as presented in the Bible. My partner in this historical sweep is my husband of forty-seven years, Henry H. Mitchell, known as a preacher, a teacher of preachers, and a writer on preaching. He declined the invitation to write a sermon for this book, but readily agreed to joint-venture the opening argument or data base of various traditions.

A brief identification of each of the other writers is printed with their sermons. But I would be remiss if I did not here express my deep gratitude for their gracious willingness to help and to struggle with specifications and deadlines.

Special thanks go to Ms. Kimberly Blackwell, my former assistant at Spelman, for her sterling work as sermon cassette transcriber; to the Rev. Dr. Anthony C. Campbell, Professor of Preaching at the Boston University School of Theology, for his original insistence that it was time for me to do a book like this; to the Rev. Richard L. Hayes and Mr. James Hopkins, who served repeatedly as computer consultants when we were desperate; to Mrs. Dorothy Gray, Mr. Thom Moyd, and our daughters, Muriel and Elizabeth, for their assistance in typing the finished drafts; and to the Rev. Susan Newman Hopkins, Chaplain at Hood College, the Rev. Martha J. Simmons, San Francisco preacher and law student, and the Rev. Prathia Hall Wynn of the faculty of the United Theological Seminary of Dayton, for their patient and efficient support with editorial details. Then, of course, my partner, Henry, has been tirelessly involved in far more than the article we wrote together. He has been a most creative editorial critic and consultant in and with all of my efforts. Finally, my unspeakable gratitude to God for the health, strength, insight, and opportunities which have so brightened my senior years, making of them quite literally "the last of life for which the first was made."

—Ella Pearson Mitchell

WOMEN:
A HISTORICAL PERSPECTIVE

ELLA PEARSON MITCHELL AND HENRY H. MITCHELL

It is always wise to look at an issue of culture in historical perspective. The yield of insight includes, first of all, the ideological direction from which society has come, with all that this might mean in terms of where we can or should go. The awareness of history also provides a vitally important understanding of how widely elaborated and deeply entrenched a traditional position might be. This is especially true of our present topic, women as preachers. A final yield is a solid basis inside a given tradition, on which to build whatever fresh understanding is projected. One seldom dares to propose anything utterly new. As Jesus said of his own tradition, "I am not come to destroy, but to fulfil" (Matthew 5:17, KJV). So this historical introduction serves the function of preparing us to deal with this book's title question of whether or not women's preaching could fulfill the goals of the Christian faith tradition and truly be within the will of God.

As one views history, however, it is never with absolute objectivity. One may feel dispassionate simply because one has a detached air. But the very questions one asks and the categories one uses belie a particular frame of reference. To be up front with the categories and assumptions used here, let us start with the fact that there is secular thought and Christian thought. The former is traced in this work for the purpose of determining just how biased a culture may have been, and what influence, if any, it may have had on Christianity in a given period. Our ultimate concern here, however, is to establish a Christian (biblically grounded) documentation for the fact that women have been and are called by God to preach.

Prior to formal religious thought, one starts at the very beginning, with the question of whether a person or a society even believes that women are fully human. We can move no further until this question is answered. Ancient society did not consider women fully human. And, as incredible as this may seem, there are manifest today residual evidences of the view of womanhood as less than fully human. It has taken an amendment to the Constitution to affirm the obvious opposite, but even that has not been adequate to eliminate the subtle survivals of the benighted concept of women as less than human. In the earliest written history studied here, secular and sacred views were identical, with the Old Testament tradition suggesting the limitations on the full humanity of women that were common to most of the thought of the time. The rare deviations were actually breakthroughs of divine revelation.

A second assumption is that there is no difference between status and role in a society. That is to say that equality before God is utterly without meaning, if it is not expressed in the equality of role, to the extent that one has the gifts to perform the role. Thus, it is no less nonsensical to say that God made men and women equal and put men only in the seats of authority, than it was to say that God was the author of the power arrangement of the slave system. In the area of secular logic, a discipline created by God, it makes no sense to say that the uniqueness of childbearing overrides for all time the high quality of the God-given intellectual, administrative, and spiritual gifts of a woman. This logic is all the more compelling when one contemplates the severe limitations on the gifts of some of the men holding authority now. God is surely not that wasteful, but that is far ahead of our story, which will conclude with the theology of gifts.

A third assumption is that there are no limitations on the efficacy of the atonement of Christ for the sins of all people. To the secular mind it is unthinkable that the salvation offered by the all-wise and just Creator should be applied selectively. To the Bible believer, it is downright heresy to suggest that John 3:16 refers to a love of God applicable to only a part of the world. And in case one wonders why this is even brought up, one has only to look at the notion that all women are under a curse established in relation to Eve (I Timothy 2:11-15), or that there is a particular *work,* childbearing, required to make grace available to women. (Compare Ephesians 2:8-9.) It is as absurd as the idea that the sons of Ham were cursed by a drunken

Noah (Genesis 9:25-27), and that God honored the curse so fully as to maintain it as an eternal exception to the promises of salvation in Christ after repentance and faith. Just as slave masters concocted these astounding theological atrocities and defended them with incredible dedication, so do both men and women today overlook the monstrous deviltry of a condition of birth (such as being born female) for which even Christ cannot overcome the "penalty." Entrenched privilege carefully picks passages out of context and presses them to the exclusion of all else, even the adequacy of salvation in Christ.

Secular intellectuals and seriously thoughtful Christians may join in wonderment at the need for these assumptions. But among those for whom we write are many persons still struggling for a way to throw off these concocted biblical justifications of less than full freedom and equal function for the female children of God. These strugglers' only hope is a no-holds-barred engagement with the illogical as well as unbiblical ideas and practices that have been so deeply entrenched in human society from antiquity.

Assumptions for the Biblical Study of the Status and Role of Women

The status of women in the Bible echoes much the same cultural direction as secular history does; yet we insist that the Bible is not ultimately self-contradictory, despite the conflicts apparent from a cursory reading. This means that serious thought will have to be given to the interpretation of the Word, and this requires rules or guidelines in the disciplines of exegesis (critical analysis) and hermeneutics (interpretation). Since rules often vary according to positions taken, they may also be referred to as assumptions. So it is fair, once again, to state up front the assumptions to be followed. The first assumption is that revelation, as well as society, is dynamic and progressive. The summit of revelation is the life, teachings, death, and resurrection of Jesus Christ. Given this final biblical revelation, it is to be understood that God *still* speaks to individuals, and our prayerful interpretation of the changeless Word can still improve. It is also understood that at least some of the biblical revelation and Christian practice following the Gospels (lives of Christ) may not have been fully representative of the radical message of Christ. This is quite within our assumptions of harmony, if we consider the hazards of institutionalization, as well as the necessities of application by and among finite human beings and groups of human beings. Revelation applies to specific contexts.

What was seen as the very will of God in Genesis is thus overridden later in the Old or New Testament. In an earlier culture, the call of God led to major improvements which, in the light of still later improvements, would not be normative today. This is certainly true of polygamy, and with it the status of women. So what was assumed to be the will of God in one historical context was overridden by progressive revelation in another.

In our insistence that the Bible is not self-contradictory, then, we are not insisting that we have to harmonize the enriching varieties of different times in history, or different places on earth. The unifying theme is that all of these people are hearing and doing the will of God to the very best of their spiritual insight, and we can learn from every single one of them. In some cases, God leads people to use admittedly imperfect indigenous culture to achieve some other, more important goal. In other cases God leads people to challenge prevailing culture, or quietly to move on beyond it.

This sort of thing is still true. We happen to believe that any serious Christians would tithe their material income without question. But if we were pastors and made tithing a mandatory prerequisite to church membership, we just might be arbitrary rather than inspired. Such was likely the case with the apostle Paul, whose task it was to stabilize Christian groups into churches for the long haul, starting from wherever they might be at the time, both spiritually and culturally. Also, he had to consider their context and what any given act might mean to the pagan world around them. So, since he worked in different places at different times, his inspired principles are bound to result in some differing instructions. in his correspondence.

We assume, then, that every passage in the Bible can only be properly interpreted in the light of all related passages in the whole of the Bible, and that culture and context are especially crucial considerations every time we try to interpret a passage in apparent contrast with some other passage. With these guidelines or assumptions in mind, we move first to the general status of women in the Bible. Building on that inseparable foundation of female role and general status, we may then deal with the specific issue of ordaining women to the professional clergy.

Women in the Old Testament

One doesn't have to look very far for the first implications concerning the status of women in the Bible. In Genesis 1:26-28, when God said "let us make man in our image, after our likeness," there followed an assignment of dominion to *"them."* Then comes the declaration that "male and female created he *them"* (KJV, italics added), with a repetition of the assignment of dominion to *"them."* In the order established at creation, the equality of male and female is quite clear.

In the next chapter (vv. 19-25), a sequence is established, with the man before the woman, but she is still bone of his bone and flesh of his flesh. He is to leave his parents and cling to her, and they are to be one; so the theme of mutuality is continued within the concept of woman having been taken out of man. The popular notion of subordination probably arises from verse 18, which states that her purpose for being is to help her husband. But the word mate is still there, and if they are seriously "one flesh," this could hardly mean subordination. One even hears God commanding Abraham to do whatever Sarah tells him, at one point (Gen. 21:12). They are indeed equal, not hierarchical.

Genesis 3, however, is the source of a radically different approach. Eve is reported to be the first transgressor, having succeeded in tempting Adam to eat the forbidden fruit. Thereby his intended domination is already compromised, but her sin is used to justify punishments such as pain in childbirth and subordination to the rule of her husband (3:16). Of course, there is no clear statement that this punishment applies to all the women of the ensuing centuries, but it has been widely construed that way.

One supposed justification would seem to be the strange, multi-generational decree of enmity "between thee and the woman, and between thy seed and her seed" (3:15, KJV). *Later* reference in even the New Testament is read to imply the application of this decree to all women for all time. Paul advises that women should learn in silence and never be allowed to have authority or teach. This is "because" Adam was formed first, and also because Eve deceived Adam. Nevertheless, women can be saved in childbearing, "if they continue in faith and charity and holiness with sobriety" (I Timothy 2:11-15, KJV).

At this point, one is reminded of our third original assumption about the sufficiency of grace, and of the reference to this passage in that connection. Paul, who was so insistent on the sufficiency of grace in Galatians and Ephesians, apparently comes to a situation where he feels it necessary to shun the very appearance of evil with regard to the role of women. Since the women of the surrounding pagan cults in Corinth had such immoral influence, he deemed it wise to assure Timothy's clarity of witness by severe restrictions on Christian women. (The same restrictions are quoted in I Corinthians 14:34-35.) As he digs into popular but not really biblical folk belief, he comes up with this thing about Eve. He probably never dreamed that this strictly contextual counsel would one day be laid alongside Galatians 3:28 (no male or female in Christ) or any of his approving mentions of examples of women engaged in prophesying and teaching. These will be discussed a little later.

We move now to Deuteronomy, where female slaves, as well as male slaves, are emancipated every seven years, if they are of the Hebrews (15:12-17). One also finds here a marvelously humane law concerning women taken prisoner in war and then taken as wives. The new wife is to be given time to mourn the loss of her parents, and then she is to take off the garments of captivity and become a full citizen, so to speak. After this, if there is a divorce, she is not to be sold as a slave (21:10-14). This law goes on to forbid inequality of inheritance, as between the children of two wives, one of whom is loved more than the other. Some semblance of humaneness and equality is undeniable here.

The law in Deuteronomy 22:22 (with parallel in Leviticus 20:10) even goes so far as to make men and women seem equally culpable in adultery, *both* being subject to death. This, again, would appear to have the earmarks of justice and equality for women. The truth, however, is that the equality of punishment is based on concern that the female property of one *male* was violated by another. Unmarried women were not covered. So the motive was not real equality, as seen when there was a choice between abuse of a male or of his concubine and his host's daughter (Judges 19:24 ff.). This sexual license of men had already been recognized in the story of Tamar, who was to be executed for being pregnant out of wedlock, while the father-in-law was without censure (Genesis 38:12-26). A father could even sell his daughter into servitude, under certain conditions (Exodus 21:7). The conditions listed bespeak a humane undercurrent, but the main thrust of the law devalues daughters. So, with only occasional exceptions, the Old Testament law was prone to place women in a very inferior position. It is hardly likely, also, that the more equalitarian and humane laws were actually enforced most of the time. Georgia Harkness, author of *Women in Church and Society,* notes astutely that the only recorded stoning for adultery was all the way over in John 8:7, and it involved a woman, not a man.

Perhaps the most telling evidence of Old Testament cultural bias against women, however, is to be found in the resounding silence of most of the prophets. The treatment of women simply was not even an issue. Isaiah 19:16 speaks figuratively of women, but they represent fear and cowardice, which is a put-down. Hosea's wife, Gomer, is certainly no credit to her gender, and Zechariah's female angels also represent evil (5:7-11). The preponderance of female figures is unmistakably evil.

The exceptions, however, are marvelous. Though Proverbs is not a book of the prophets as such, it uses women to personify wisdom. This book even proposes that women engage in business (31:10-31), to an extent not found anywhere else, and not likely to have prevailed. Yet the male is still the dominant figure, and everything in this partially liberated woman's life is to his glory and profit.

We conclude this Old Testament consideration with the exceptional people whose lives contradicted the prevailing trends—rare women of great role and recognition. The first of these, of course, predates the Deuteronomic Law, but surely comes after the Genesis account, which was used centuries later to suppress women in the two instances cited involving Paul. Her name was Miriam, and she was a prophetess. She led the singing for her brother Moses, but she must also have taught. It is quite significant that Micah (6:4) reports God reminding the Israelites that they were given Moses, Aaron, and *Miriam,* to *lead* them out of the land of Egypt. Notwithstanding her later rebellion against Moses' leadership, and her bias against his Ethiopian wife, she was indeed recognized as a major leader, one on the team of three.

The next woman to burst the bonds of the traditional limits on women was Deborah, well known as a military leader and ruling judge, but also a spiritual leader and "prophetess" (Judges 4:4). She was a popular counselor, the governor-judge, and the leader of the triumphant army. Rabbinical tradition has it that this "super-woman" rose from the lowly estate of lamp keeper in the tabernacle. Though women's biographies were not considered important, her own merit and performance as counselor, judge, and seer was so impressive that the populace forgot her gender. The esteem in which she was held is demonstrated by the fact that Barak, general of the army, would not dare to face battle against the superior Sisera without her at his side. (It is important to note that no mention is made of the fact that Deborah's womanhood was a major exception to the rules, which may, thus, have been far less important than is often assumed.)

Perhaps the most significant female for our purposes here is Huldah, the woman whose advice was so seriously sought by King Josiah. The temple worship had ceased and the place was in ruins. Some scrolls suspected of containing the Law were found in the temple debris by Hilkiah the high priest. When they were presented to young King Josiah, he wanted to be sure the scrolls were authentic, and not the work of an imposter. He sent a delegation of five of his highest court officials to consult with Huldah, who alone could be trusted to know the real from the fictitious in such matters. The record (II Chronicles 34:22; II Kings 22:14) is typical of its day, describing Huldah only as the wife of Shallum, since women had no importance in their own right. The only information we are given about her is the fact that she lived near the temple and palace, where her husband was keeper of the king's wardrobe. Tradition suggests that she was a teacher. In any case, her evaluation of the documents and her declaration of the wrath of God on their idolatry were taken most seriously. And when a woman is rated over the high priest in judging crucial spiritual matters, it has to be obvious that God places no limitations on what a woman can do. This is true all the more when God has already prepared her and continues to work through her.

The Old Testament, then, has a preponderance of traditional limitations on women, but the divinely ordained breakthroughs of equality are sufficiently numerous to make a modern believer aware that God is never without some witness for the highest values in the divine will. In fact, it can all be summed up in the relatively early declaration in Exodus that the whole nation shall be a kingdom of priests (Exodus 19:6). There will be no need to have anyone to mediate between God and either male or female. This is the ultimate equality, and this surely applies to the priesthood (professional ministry) of women.

Women in the New Testament

We move now to an emphasis on the traditional treatment of women in the New Testament era and following, including the early church and the church "fathers." The three main areas of concern are women in the ministry of our Lord, women in the New Testament church (especially the thought of Paul), and women in the life and thought of the church during the first five centuries. In the first two, we shall be deeply involved in the biblical record, while the third will focus primarily on the writings of the leaders and thinkers through Augustine (A.D. 354-430).

Many women figured in the ministry of Jesus, both among those he healed and those who followed closely and watched over and supported the labors. Jesus also had no problem with frequently referring to women in the parables, as they made bread, looked for a lost coin, etc. He attended weddings and made use of the wedding metaphor in positive ways. He may have refrained from marriage earlier because of his role as older son in a family where the father had died. He made no direct pronouncement on the treatment of women as such, but his many experiences with them bespeak an openness and love without restrictions of any kind.

There were no women in the official twelve disciples, but this would have been an embarrassment, given their itinerant lifestyle and closeness. The women who did follow had to be organized for their own protection (both safety and reputation) in a separate band, and there is no indication that they could afford to be with Jesus at all times, as were the official twelve.

Jesus' affirmation of and commitment to women, however, was so complete that he went repeatedly against tradition on their behalf. He had little concern for what people thought, as he chatted easily with the Samaritan woman at the well (John 4:1-30). John reports him to be equally open to and caring for the woman about to be stoned for adultery (8:3-11). He actually pointed out the unjust absurdity of blaming the female and saying nothing to the male transgressors. When a known prostitute intimately washed his feet and dried them with her hair, actually kissing them, Jesus told a whole parable in her defense and pronounced her forgiven and saved (Luke 7:37-50).

When women deserved high praise or encouragement, Jesus had no qualms about giving it, regardless of popular sentiment. The Syrophoenician woman was praised for her superior faith (Mark 7:26-30). A diseased and scared woman was encouraged, regardless of her lawbreaking daring in moving about in public and touching the hem of Jesus' robe in her "unclean" condition (Mark 5:34 and Luke 8:48). A woman bent over for eighteen years was thought in the minds of many to be thus for her sins, but Jesus promptly healed her, with no questions asked (Luke 13:11-13). The full humanity of women was unequivocally affirmed by everything Jesus said and did.

Jesus' example goes even further; he was very closely attached to women like Mary and Martha of Bethany. It was in their home that he sought rest and relaxation in his most stressful final week of witness, before the crucifixion. He affirmed Mary's spiritual inquisitiveness, but he also affirmed Martha's feminine domesticity and the service it represented.

In fact, Jesus' ideas about what it takes to be great had no notion of subordination of anybody at all to anybody else. Such a hierarchy as men over women would be exactly opposite what Jesus said to his own disciples: "Ye know that the princes of the Gentiles exercise dominion over them, and they that are great exercise authority upon them. But it shall not be so among you: but whosoever will be great among you, let him be your minister; and whosoever will be chief among you, let him be your servant" (Matthew 20:25-27, KJV). He said also that he would not call his disciples servants, but friends (John 15:15).

So a sweeping differentiation between served and servants was far from the mind of Christ. In fact, his community of witness had no discrimination. Although it was widely assumed that respectable women did not take part in public life, Jesus welcomed them to his activities, drawing one of his first crowds of seekers by means of the pioneering evangelism of the woman at the well in Samaria. He welcomed the fact that women like Mary and Joanna followed him all the way from Nazareth to Jerusalem, providing the only financial contributions of which we have any record. It was the courage bestowed by Jesus that enabled the women to be the last at the cross and the first at the tomb, thus becoming the first to know and announce the resurrection. In the light of Jesus' openness to and concern for women, their place in the first churches was unprecedentedly prominent. We move now to examine that place.

In the upper room prayer vigil, women were clearly a part of the church aborning, including Mary, the mother of Jesus (Acts 1:14). There seems to be no evidence that they voted on Judas' replacement, but they were fully involved when Joel's prophecy was fulfilled and women were filled with the spirit and prophesied (Acts 2:17). When the church expanded into the homes (Acts 2:46-47), the women were certainly present and active as more than hostesses.

When Paul wrote the church at Rome, he mentioned twenty-nine of his co-workers in the ministry of the church, ten of whom were women. Whatever else he may have said to Timothy or anybody else about the specific situation at the troubled congregation in Corinth, he was deeply engaged with the female leadership of many other ministries. His strongest support came from the church at Philippi, founded on women and led by the gifted businesswoman and church organizer, Lydia. The language used to describe these women is the same as that used to describe the male leaders, and there is no reason to suspect that Paul was congratulating them with tongue in cheek.

The Priscilla mentioned in Romans 16:3 is the same co-worker with whom Paul worked as tentmaker, along with her husband Aquila. It was she, apparently more than her husband, who learned so much of Paul's teaching that she was mentioned first in the assignment of this couple to the task of instructing the gifted but theologically deficient evangelist, Apollos (Acts 18:26). She would surely have wondered at a blanket application of Paul's word to Timothy about women not being allowed to teach in Corinth or Ephesus or wherever, for specifically local reasons (I Timothy 2:11-12).

In addition to the apparent limitations of these restrictive sayings to local situations, there is the problem of accurately translating specific words. The oppression of women is found to occur in some cases because the English translations do not reflect the original meaning. Take for instance the word for head used in Ephesians 5:21-23, the Greek *kephale.* Here the head is the source as opposed to the authority, and the meaning has to do with the responsibility of the husband, not the dictatorial power. Major studies have been done on this word for head, all of them suggesting that we have to use the meaning it had *then,* not the present metaphorical meaning of that same word.[1] Even the word "submit" is misunderstood, by the simple expedient of forgetting to read it in verse 21. Here it is *mutual* submission, and it sets the meaning of that verb in verse 22, where it is omitted and taken for granted in many early versions.

First Timothy 2:11-12 speaks in the King James Version of women learning in "silence," when the real meaning would be more like "calm" or "quietness." The word for the "authority" usurped over men is used in no other place in the New Testament, and its meaning is more like the word "domineering." With that understanding the advice is still good for any church, and it works both ways, with men also well advised not to domineer women.[2]

The place of women in the early church is further complicated by what appears to be an easy willingness for them to preach or prophesy in some places, but not to have any real authority. Just as the women at Jerusalem had no vote on Judas' successor, because they had not been official disciples, women continued to be very active without being mentioned as heads of any group. This is with the possible exception of Lydia at Philippi. Dorcas is given the title of "disciple" (Acts 9:36), and Philip the evangelist had four virgin daughters who prophesied (Acts 21:9). But the sensitivity to women ever having any power, which is undeniably underneath the restrictions in I Timothy, has continued to this very day. As recently as July 29, 1990, Wyatt T. Walker, pastor and celebrated civil rights leader during the era of Martin Luther King, Jr., was reported in *The New York Times* as saying that many young women were better at preaching than at routine working with congregants. While he maintained that ambitious women preachers were not interested in the day-to-day details and duties, he implied that they would not handle administration (authority) well. The prognosis for the transition to female preachers and assistants is far better than the prospects for them to be given substantial authority—this despite a few beginning bishops in denominations such as the United Methodists and the Episcopalians.

Notwithstanding all these often subtle limitations on women, the

[1]Berkeley & Alvera Mickelson, "What Does Kephale Mean in the New Testament?" in *Women, Authority & the Bible,* ed. Alvera Mickelson (Downers Grove, Illinois: Inter-Varsity Press, 1986), pp. 97–110.

[2]"A Biblical and Theological Basis for Women in Ministry," a pamphlet of Covenant Publications (Chicago, 1987), p. 6.

fact is that the place of women was never really an open issue. Paul, who fought valiantly for full equality for the Gentiles (Compare Galatians 3:28; Colossians 3:11), did not sense a similar need in regard to women. The freedom of activity and expression that they had was enough to mask the depth of the cultural bias. And what he may have viewed casually as quite acceptable treatment of women becomes even commendable in comparison to the diminished roles assigned women by the fathers of the church of the next centuries.

Church Women in the Patristic Period and
on to the Reformation

The African church father, Tertullian (160?-230?), said little about women as such, except strongly to support and enlarge Paul's instruction that women be clothed conservatively in worship (I Timothy 2:9). Jerome (340?-420), the Latin scholar at Rome, agreed with Tertullian in viewing sex as sinful and women as the seducers of men to engage in sex.[3] Clement of Alexandria (150?-220?) was little better, with a word only to the effect that dresses cover women's knees.

Augustine (354-430) was perhaps the most important influence of all on subsequent treatment of women. He may be summarized thus: Since sex was so important in his pre-conversion rebellion, he was prone ever after to view it as sinful. Thus, although he was more positive about marriage than other church fathers, it was not as good in his eyes as celibacy. He returned to the old Roman idea of the father's role in the family as that of inflicting physical punishment on wives as well as children; woman's threefold role was as temptress, wife, and mother. It was Augustine more than Paul or any other influential Christian leader who invented the idea of sexuality as inherently tainted with evil.[4]

Thomas Aquinas (1225?-74), the great theologian, was not so extreme, but was heavily influenced by Augustine, and the Roman Catholic Church still reflects the dualism of flesh and spirit so prominent in Augustine. The Protestant Reformation threw off many yokes of oppression and error, but not this one. "Neither Luther nor Calvin gave a thought to the equality of women as persons."[5] Both

[3]Georgia Harkness, *Women in Church and Society* (Nashville: Abingdon Press, 1972), p. 197.
[4]Harkness, pp. 195–199, and Agonito, pp. 73–74.
[5]Harkness, p. 83.

married, but neither wife was more than a subordinate.

Two forms of female rebellion emerged. One was the formation of women Catholics into convents, where women could exercise their gifts under other women, learning, teaching, and ministering in a manner still worthy of respect and admiration. The first of these convents was begun in the fourth century. Protestant rebellion among women has been limited to small sects, often organized by themselves, and to such unconventional groups as the Quakers, who have no professional ordained clergy, male or female. There was no seriously notable progress in the role of women until the nineteenth and twentieth centuries.

Women in the Church of the
Last Two Centuries

The current widespread debates on the role of women can be traced to courageous advocates such as Abigail Smith Adams (1744–1818), Mary Wollstonecraft (1759–1797), Emma Hart Willard (1787–1870), Sojourner Truth (1797–1883), Mary Lyon (1797–1849), and Catherine Beecher (1800–1878). Abigail Adams wrote her husband in the White House to say that women would refuse to be bound by laws and a constitution in whose making they had no part. Even so, it was not until *1920* that the Women's Rights Movement, organized in 1848, was successful in winning an amendment to the Constitution which awarded women the minimal recognition of the vote.

Women as far back as Emma Willard started "seminaries" for the training of women, and slowly but surely they were moved to what is now a kind of educational and professional parity with men. But it must not be forgotten that female genius, now so prominent in many of the disciplines, was unrecognized and actually legally excluded until relatively recently. The role of women as ministers was only one of many options that were arbitrarily denied. Early women ministers of great stature, such as Lucretia Collins Mott (1793–1880), Elizabeth Cady Stanton (1816–1902), Lucy Stone Blackwell (1818–1893), and Susan B. Anthony (1820–1906) were never ordained, but they preached and paved the way.

The sweep of history is thus seen to be full of obstacles and oppression for the women who knew themselves to be called of God to preach, but the will of God cannot be forever thwarted. The tide in the United States seems to have begun to turn around 1920, along with the success of the suffrage movement. Even at that pivotal point in history there were reported to be already more than three thousand female ministers and preachers in the country.[6] The number today is vastly more, with many theological seminaries reporting more female than male students.

Furthermore, it is apparent that many of the women enrolled are very gifted. Our own experience in one seminary saw six out of eight classes led academically by women, even though the percent of females in the class was less than ten at the time. If placement of such gifted women were on the basis of capability, whether by the episcopate or by congregational vote, our title's question would be moot, and the churches of Christ would be unprecedentedly blessed. But there is hardly any discernible trend in that direction even now. The track to senior pastorates in larger congregations, after apprenticeships as assistants and distinguished service in smaller churches, is only beginning to be manifest.

This raises our concluding topic, the doctrine or theology of the gifts God bestows on male and female alike.

A Concluding Theology of Gifts

To sum up the thrust of this brief history it seems abundantly evident that God has definitively burst through and beyond the deeply entrenched bias of earlier eras and incarnated in Jesus Christ a pattern for all time. The most important characteristics of Jesus' earthly ministry were grace and compassion, justice and equality, and the freedom to become fulfilled children of God. To follow these principles today, rather than to adhere to specific, localized advice of Paul and others, would liberate women in the church, to live and serve with equal opportunity to employ their God-given talents in the vocations for which the talents were given in the first place. It is this concern for gifts which constitutes the crux of our concluding theological response to the question of our title, *Women: To Preach or Not to Preach?*

Three representative passages of Scripture form the main basis of this brief theological approach, but the whole of Jesus' rules for the kingdom are involved directly or indirectly. Jesus' most direct statement on the God-given gifts is to be found in the well-known para-

---

[6]Harkness, p. 129.

ble of the talents. (Matthew 25:14-30). The apostle Paul's most direct statement is in I Corinthians 12, especially verse 4: "Now there are diversities of gifts, but the same Spirit" (KJV). He was seeking to blend the gifts or talents of a diverse group into one functioning corpus, the body of Christ, the church. The third is Paul's most succint and important statement on women, which is to the effect that in Christ is neither male nor female (Galatians 3:28). It is ironic that two minor local applications (I Corinthians 14:34 and I Timothy 2:11-14) of what Paul might have considered commonsense exceptions, should have gained such credence and support among the privileged male power bloc. Even more ironic is the fact that these exceptions are used by so many of all groups to set aside the universal principles of Jesus' ministry mentioned above.

Arguing from minor exceptions, society's majority has for nearly two thousand years set aside the will of Christ and the principles of the kingdom, to preserve an ancient injustice. The only doctrine or theological argument ever raised by Paul to support the local variances advised is manifestly early Old Testament and superseded, as Paul knew very well, by the revelation in Christ. The reference to Eve in I Timothy 2:13-15 is a contradiction of the doctrine of salvation by faith (Ephesians 2:8) and the atonement of Christ (John 3:16).

Let us conclude, then, with the biblical theology of the gifts of God to all of God's children. In Christ there is no distinction between them. The actual distribution of gifts is the most concrete evidence possible that God is no respecter of persons (Acts 10:34). We the authors, as members of an ethnic minority in America, rejoice repeatedly to see the astonishing genius of a child born in a modern manger. We see also, as teachers of homiletics, that God's gifts are not predictably associated with any one group. In Christ the gifts of preaching are spread all over. In a largely African American class in preaching, the best narrative sermon presented was by one of two white students. The rest of us had to confront the strengths of our culture applied superbly by the gifts of a person of another culture, because God's gifts follow none of our rules and expectations.

In an intensive workshop on preaching held for midwestern Catholics, two women not normally assigned to do the homilies in the Mass were far and away the fastest to learn and use the preaching principles being taught. These had to do with communicating with the *whole* of a person, not just the cognitive consciousness, as Western culture has been prone to do until relatively recently. Like almost all women, these nuns had been brought up to be more sensitive to feelings and intuitions than most men are. It was no mystery that they made better communicators with the whole of the human psyche. Their gifts are typical of thousands of women. God can use those gifts since there is no male or female in Christ. If society has engaged in a special type of social formation for girls, this original bias has been used providentially to prepare them for a much needed renaissance in the American pulpit.

Paul's word to the Corinthian church was that the church is best served when each of the gifted respects and works with all the rest of the gifted. It is not healthy for the body to have parts which despise the other parts, no matter how unsightly, as he said in First Corinthians 12:23. Whatever the previous patterns of relationships and of the expression of gifts, in the body of Christ the members are one body, each doing what it was created by God to do. And one knows what that calling is by the very capacity to perform a given task. This, of course, includes preaching.

Finally, Jesus insists that gifts must not be wasted. The Parable of the Talents speaks of the harsh judgment made on a person who through cowardice, laziness, envy, or misconception, failed to use what was assigned or entrusted. One wonders what the judgment will be against those who arbitrarily prevent persons from exercising their talents, frustrating both the Creator and the gifted preacher created.

The Christian churches of America, both Catholic and Protestant, stand at a critical point in history. The membership trends, except in unconventional and of the denominationally unconnected ministries, is down. The Bible is not the living power it was in the days of the First and Second Great Awakenings, because it is not preached with warmth and vivid power. Yet the gifts needed to restore the Bible to its rightful place are abundantly available, both among women and among men bestirred to preach with power by a new and fruitful mix of cultures and genders. It is time to unleash what Socrates would have called a half of the talents of the church, for her renewal, and for the salvation of the world.

DON'T BE ASHAMED

TEXT: Romans 1:16

You have some good news.

The word "gospel" is the English translation of the Greek *eu-ang-gellion,* which means "beautiful message" or "good news." As God-called preachers, you have some good news for us, and we want to hear it. Notice that I have said "good news" and not just "true news." All true news is not good news. The facts may be too painful to take. The truth may be too tragic to face, because naked truth, without love, stands helplessly before mysteries it cannot fathom, and people it cannot help, things that it cannot change, problems that it cannot solve, and sins that it cannot forgive. Paul said, "Tell the truth in *love.''*

And so, you have more than true news, you have good news, soul-saving news, mind-liberating news, burden-lifting, heart-fixing, fellowship-creating news; people-empowering, joy-inspiring, earth-redeeming, world-reconciling, problem-solving news.

It is not *your* news. You did not create it; you can only proclaim it. You didn't make it; you can only deliver it. You didn't write it; you can only take down the divine dictation and put it in your language. And you would not have done even that, if you had not been chosen by the head of God's news agency, to receive and transmit the dictation.

God maintains control over God's own news agency. God knows

Charles G. Adams is Senior Pastor of Hartford Memorial Baptist Church in Detroit, Michigan, and President of the Progressive National Baptist Convention.
Note: This message was preached at the ordination of Jeanette Pollard at Hartford Memorial Baptist Church in Detroit, Michigan.

what to say and whom God would choose to say what God wants said. It is not for me or for any church or any denominational leadership to decide whom God would use in "God's news agency." It is not for us to say whom we want to hear, or from whom we want to receive the message, because the Good News does not compel us to believe in the messenger, only to accept the message. It is not for us to say that we don't want to hear an African preacher, or an Arab preacher, or a woman preacher, because we are not the head of the news agency. God will choose whom God will to advance what God said, and it must never be our place to block somebody else from a position in a news agency that does not belong to us.

We don't know it all. We can't do it all. We can't tell it all. But, I'm just glad to be allowed to say something here today. I'm just glad that while God was choosing others that God also chose me, and God chose you. How can people call on a God of whom they have not heard? And how can they hear without a preacher? And how can the preacher preach unless the preacher has been sent? Sent by whom? Who else but the head of the news agency?

God creates the news, controls the news, fulfills and directs the news agency. And ordination is not going to give you anything that you don't already have. We only recognize and celebrate what God has already done for you.

Don't be ashamed of the good news of God, because it is not your news. It is not about you; it is the power of God unto salvation. Wouldn't it be a terrible thing for you and me to have to tell folks about something that we are ashamed of—something that we feel bad about—because we don't want the bad news to fall from our lips, to discourage or destroy or devastate another human being? But since it isn't *our* Good News, since it is God's Good News, we can feel good, because God has given us the privilege to tell it.

And I want you to be proud. I want you to let it wake you up in the middle of the night. I want you to let it push you out into the streets, and tell everybody that you've got some Good News from the Lord—that there is a balm in Gilead to make the wounded whole. Tell everybody that there is a solution to every problem, there is a light that can guide us, there is a power that can keep us, there is a Lord that can lift us, there is a grace that can save us, there is a hope that can hold us, there is a truth that can set us free, there is a love that can never let us go. Don't be ashamed to tell the Good News.

Well, Goodspeed says that a better translation of the text is that you should be proud. I want you to be proud, not of your own achievements, but because you are what you are by the grace of God. Proud not because of your self-sufficiency, because every day of your ministry you will have to depend on God. Proud not because of what you have done, because you could not have done it unless God had done it through you. But, I want you to be proud because God has made you, because God has saved you, and because the Holy Ghost has blessed you. Proud because God sent you, God called you, God raised you, God healed you, God delivered you, God brought you through all kinds of adversities. Proud because God touched you.

And why shouldn't you be proud? Well, be proud because of the positive nature of the gospel. The gospel comes in a powerful form of encouragement and reassurance. It is not condemnation; it is regeneration. It is not judgment; it is judgment wrapped in grace. Now of course there are some sins that must be condemned; some injustices must be corrected. There is some bad news of evil that must be dealt with by the Good News of salvation. But that is not the main motif of the gospel. The main motif of the gospel may include judgment, but it isn't judgment; it is grace.

Now, when we preach, we must never preach to exclude or accuse anyone, but to include, inspire, encourage everyone. That means that we ourselves must never take ourselves to be God or to be perfect. We are only fellow travelers in an imperfect world full of imperfect people, ourselves included. So the gospel is not about us. God did not tell us to stand up and hold ourselves up as examples. We're here to say that we all have sinned and fallen short of the grace of God, and that God still loves us.

So let our gospel go in search of the residual goodness that is found in all people, even sinful people. Martin Luther King, Jr., believed in the essential goodness of human beings, even his persecutors. We must always look upon people as sinners saved by grace, and the demons within them are alien to their true selves. That means that there is something good in everybody, and the gospel has to search hard to find it. The Good News of God predominates over the bad news of people. So be proud. The bad news is that we have sinned; the Good News is that Christ is the Savior. So be proud of the power of the gospel to reform and save.

Secondly, be proud of the personal and perfect content of the gospel. The gospel is more than appearance; it is a solid reality. Many positive forms hide negative contents. The right sound does not always make the right sense. Jesus said, "Not every one that saith unto me, Lord, Lord, shall enter into the kingdom of heaven; but he that doeth the will of my Father which is in heaven" (Matthew 7:21, KJV).

Religious talk is the most cruelly deceptive of all forms of speech, if it is not sincere. If everybody who talks religious were to walk really religious, the world would be a paradise. I think of what Jesus said when he quoted Isaiah 29:13, "These people honor me with their lips, but their hearts are far from me" (Matthew 15:8, NIV). The Good News of God has not only a comely form, but a compassionate center.

The gospel does not mislead, does not disappoint, does not deceive. Love is the core of it, Christ is the content of it, truth is the center of it, God is the chief actor of it, salvation is the action of it, and the Holy Ghost is the strength of it. It is not public relations news. It is not mass media news. It is not exaggerated news. It is not made-up news; it is factual, actual, and historical news. The news is all about what God is doing. It sets wrong things right; it makes bad people good; and it makes dead folks come to a new life with God. The gospel is the Good News of what God has done and what God is doing to save the creature and transform the creation. The gospel is the proclamation and the demonstration of the mighty action of God. It declares that we are made in God's own likeness, so everybody has the liberty to think, speak, act, create and walk with God. And our walk with our Creator more than verifies the Good News that all power is still in our Lord's hands.

Be proud of the Good News; it will satisfy your every need. It will correct every wrong. Be proud, it is not only purposeful but it is also personal. It is not a statement about the Redeemer; it is not an abstraction about redemption; it is about an encounter with the Redeemer. Job did not say, "I know that my redemption is correct." He said, "I know that my redeemer lives." It is about the power of salvation. It's *Good* News; be proud of it.

And I also want you to be proud of the universal scope of the gospel. It reaches all the way around the world. From the deepest hell to the highest heaven, nobody is beyond the reach of it. Everybody is within the grasp of it. Nowhere is off-limits to the God who made

everywhere. Nobody is out of reach to a God who has made everybody. Nobody can escape from God. I don't care where they go, they
can't escape from God. Everywhere you turn, God is there.

Be proud, also, of the power and effects of what you are going to
preach, because what you are going to preach is the power of God
unto salvation, not just liberation, not just reconciliation but *salvation.*
Reconciliation without salvation is empty. Liberation without salvation can become violent. But when salvation becomes the major
burden of the Good News, God uses it for redemption, transformation, and everlasting life. People will be made whole because you
have spread the Good News.

Be proud of the Good News because God is the way through all
of our difficulties. My sister, don't be ashamed of the gospel; be
proud that you have been called to preach the gospel. Be proud that
you have found the hand of God in your poverty and adversity, in
your struggles as a student. When you decided to go to seminary,
with no guarantee of anything from anybody, God opened doors for
you and raised up friends to stand by and see you through. Be glad
that you have been called to preach the gospel. Be proud of the
gospel; it is the power of God unto salvation. It is the eternally fresh
and ever-interesting Good News!

SURPRISE!
SURPRISE!
SURPRISE!

JOHN W. KINNEY

TEXT: Luke 24:10-12, 21-24

Life is full of surprises. Some of those surprises can be painful and disappointing, but a life without surprises would soon become boring, humdrum, and meaningless. In a very real sense there would be no getting up tomorrow. For every time we wait to see the light of a new day, the eastern sun peeps over the horizon and says, "Surprise! The darkness is passing by." Surprise is essential to the energy and passion of life. As long as there is surprise, there is hope and promise in every situation. As long as I can be surprised, there is something to dream for, something to hope for, and something to reach for. This is the case in our text.

Let us peer for a moment into the fellowship of followers who are blanketed in the darkness of shattered expectations, broken dreams, and despairing grief. The men had gone off in sadness to commiserate in their brokenheartedness, to formulate a plan for the future, and, perhaps, to determine if they had a viable program. They may also have discussed who would be in charge.

Some of the women, however, had not finished caring for One who had cared so much for them. Whether this was the expected, defined role of women in the funeral process, I don't know. What is important is that even in their grief, these women felt a sincere need to finalize separation, and go to the tomb and express their love. Their devotion and care were made tangible by the spices they had pre-

John W. Kinney is Dean and Professor of Theology, School of Theology, Virginia Union University and Pastor of the Ebenezer Baptist Church in Beaver Dam, Virginia.

Note: This message was preached at the ordination of Margaret Nelson at Greater Corinth Baptist Church in San Antonio, Texas.

pared. They had not gone to the tomb expecting their responsibility in the fellowship to be altered. They did not go with a conscious desire or a premeditated plan to become the messengers of Good News to a confused fellowship and a disoriented world. They had come to love someone in whom they had experienced a redeeming, enabling, life-giving presence. But what you find out sometimes in life is that continued proximity can lead to unanticipated intimacy.

Hear me now, if you stay in somebody's company long enough and care enough, pretty soon you can find yourself confronted with an altered relationship. While they were there to show love, they were called to a serious job "in the way." The head of the company gave them a commission and a call that contradicted the assigned role of those who *thought* they ran the company. When the women went to the tomb, all of a sudden they found their status in the company altered. God sent the Spirit and said, "Not only do I thank you for loving him, but I've got something for you to do. In your love, I want you to go back to a world that thinks he's dead. I want you to go back to men and women and tell it over the mountains and hills and everywhere, 'He lives! He lives! Christ Jesus lives today! Surprise! Surprise! Surprise!'

"He is not dead; remember what he promised, 'If I be lifted up, I'll draw all people unto me' " (John 12:32, paraphrased).

I have known for a long time a dear sister who was in the church. And she was just hanging around the company, doing what she could do to help the Lord's work. But about six years ago God said, "You've been close to me, and I want to change your assignment. You have a commission in the United States Air Force, but I want to give you a commission in God's army. I am going to give a charge to you." She fought God's commission and didn't want to sign up for four years, but two years ago she said, "Lord, write my name on the roll. Sign me up; I will accept the charge that you have given me." I know she was not planning to do that. Of course, she hadn't thought about doing that, but all of a sudden the power of God came upon her, and she had a charge to keep and a God to glorify. Surprise! Surprise! Surprise!

Let's look again at the women of our Bible account. When they came back to the company with their new charge from God, those who liked to play God determined that the women could not be telling the truth. There was a problem with the message that these women brought to the church.

The first problem was that it did not fit the men's expectations. They said that it seemed like gossip, idle tales, funny woman-talk, that off-the-wall stuff women do sometimes when they get a little spiritual enthusiasm. But it was foolishness to them. (Some translations say that it was nonsense.) Why? Well, the men controlled the definition of what it meant to be faithful and who could be faithful. "We thought he was going to be the one, but we were disappointed. He has been three days dead, and one more day there will be no more hope, because decomposition will have set in." In other words, these women were saying something that did not compute with the data banks of the men's consciousness. "We saw him die; we saw him taken down from the tree; we saw him being laid in a borrowed tomb; and now you funny-talking women have the nerve to come and tell us after all we saw with our own eyes that he lives!"

You have to realize sometimes that people will not receive the message of truth, because they are defined by the world to the extent that they are limited by the world's constructions, rather than liberated by God's possibilities. You see, sometimes we need a transcendent breakthrough, a metanoyia of consciousness, a conversion of mind, a deconstruction of mentality, so we can begin to see and recognize, in spite of the human definition, in spite of scientific construction, that with God all things are possible!

Not only did the message surprise the disciples; it confused them, because it did not come through the right medium. It was polluted by the fact that the message came through the wrong vehicle. In other words, "It's the wrong message." But if what they were saying *were* possible, it surely would not have been spoken by a woman. The bearer of truth would have been a man, since men were the only ones who could know and speak such truth.

What do you do in a predicament like this? What most of us do is run back to the community that supports our own understanding. We run right back to the same folk who will reinforce our own inability to accept God's divine inbreaking. So rather than turn to God, we turn to the folk who think like we do and say: "Tell me again, that *is* foolishness that they are talking, ain't it?" Therefore, rather than turning to God's Word, they accept their own definition and say, "It must be idle tales."

I had the experience once of sharing in a conversation with a group of persons that included a woman who was preparing for ministry. One of the men there said, "Listen, sister, do you believe in the Bible?" She said, "Why, of course I do!" He said, "Well, we can stop this conversation right now." "Why?" she said. He responded, "The Bible says that women should be silent; we should not suffer a woman to teach or let her usurp authority over the man (I Timothy 2:12). You believe it; I believe it; the Bible said it. That settles it. Let's quit talking about this and move on."

Now she was a very gifted woman, so she got into exegesis and analysis of Scripture texts. She said, "Now wait a minute! You pulled out your text; let me pull out mine. Let's deal with the whole Word!" Then he said, "No! No! No! What does the Bible say? The Bible says, 'Be silent.'" She said, "The Bible didn't say that; Paul said that." They went round and round. Finally I just raised a question. "Do you feel that you are treating this woman the way that Jesus would treat her?" And he said, "I'm not talking about Jesus; what does the *Bible* say?"

This is the attitude that many of us have. We are not concerned about God's truth as it is revealed in Jesus. We are not concerned about the whole Word of God. We are concerned about our own little traditions and our made-up minds. If we were really to read the Bible, we would find as early as the creation story in Genesis 2:24 that man and woman are to be as one flesh.

Where did we get this idea that the man is over the woman? When we turn to Genesis 3:16, it says that because of the woman's sin the man shall "rule over" her. Now we've got to make up our minds in the church. Are we going to preach what God intended, "that the two shall be one," or are we going to preach what sin caused, as if Christ had never had anything to do with the sins of all of us? Are you going to preach God or are you going to preach sin? Read it! The reality is that we are so comfortable with our traditions, so comfortable with the ego investments we have in keeping things as they are, we don't run to Jesus, we run to each other.

Peter ran to Jesus, and he found out that what the women were saying was true. Surprise, surprise, surprise!

In other words, what the church needs to do today is stop debating tradition and run to Jesus! We need to position ourselves where the women sit, and if you sit where they sit you might see what they see.

When Peter went where the women had been, he understood what they were talking about: he lives! He was not in the tomb any more. They were telling the truth.

So look what happened when he positioned himself where the women were. It not only changed his assessment of the medium of women, it changed the character of his message. You see, what we are witnessing in the church is perhaps a transformation of the message of the church that will have redeeming power for the whole world. If we don't receive that message, we will be serving a Jesus who is still locked up in a tomb, rather than a Jesus who lives and sets us free.

But there remains a problem. If you read closely, it says, "*Some* of us went and found out what the women had said was true" (Luke 24:24, paraphrased). The problem is that a lot of people aren't going to see. Therefore, they still understand women as being bearers of idle tales. They have not been surprised yet.

So let us deal for a little while with the choices women have in responding to that situation. What do you do when you are a member of a company where God has given you truth and the other members of the company receive your message as idle woman talk? The first thing is to remember that you are not called to serve men; you are called to serve God. When you force yourself to embrace all of the categories of ministry as defined by maleness, you are making maleness the rule of your existence, and you give support to what has been going on in the church all along.

God wants to use you as you are and to work through who you are. What has been missing is your story, and if you don't tell your story, the church will stay in the same place it has always been. God wants you to offer your identity to the church and to offer what the Lord has done through your experience and your exposure. You've got a message that can help heal the church and this world.

This is vitally important. We often make a mistake, in that we behold in the church an unbiblical hierarchy and try to please the powers that be. Jesus calls us all friends, not servants (John 15:15). It is not his will that we walk over or on, but walk *with* our brothers and sisters in him. The spiritual model of relationship is one plus one equals one. The two shall become one. That's a spiritual fact. But what we require is that somebody be a zero. Sister, don't let anyone make you a zero, in order for the church to be one. If the church is going to be one, we need you and all the rest of the sisters to be one, also.

Then if you don't change your identity, what do you do? All too often, women change their message. In other words, they say "they won't listen to me because I am a woman, and I am saying something different. Therefore, since I can't change my biological identity, I'll change my message. I'll say what they want to hear." Please don't compromise the message in order to get the affirmation of men. Don't ever be tempted to say that women are second-class and inferior, or that they are made to be ruled over! They are made to be loved, cared for, and lived with, just as women love and care for and live with men. All of us are made for oneness, not hierarchy, to walk together in God.

Sometimes, when you find a woman who preaches the truth in the church, her worst enemies are other women. Why? Because that is the epitome of victimization, where victims become the staunch supporters of the system that victimizes them. The reason that they do not want to hear the truth is that they have worked out their little comfort zone in oppression, and they don't want another woman rocking their boat. If you are going to have a part in the saving of this world, your gospel will have to include all of the gospel truth, and let the chips fall where they may. God will do the deliverance. You don't change the message to suit men and you don't change it to suit women. Be instant in season and out of season.

I thank God that there are some women who are standing up for the Lord, and rising up in spite of doors closed in their faces, saying, "Surprise, the Savior lives! Surprise! The Savior touched my life and called me! Surprise, there is entrusted to me an important part of the living Word! Surprise, surprise, surprise!"

FAITH THAT DEFIES THE CONTEXT

W. FRANKLYN RICHARDSON

TEXT: Isaiah 40:4

I once kept a commitment to preach at a service even though I was invited by the World Council of Churches to be in Zimbabwe, with Nelson Mandela. At first I was not sure why the Lord led me to do that, but I went on. Later, I got a call from a newspaper reporter, and he said to me that some of my brothers and colleagues were upset that I was preaching in a service where a woman was being installed. Then I knew why God wanted me to be there, because beyond specific locations and personalities, the same thing that was going on in South Africa was going on there that night in Dayton.

So I was happy to be where the Lord wanted me to be. I have been blessed by that preacher's preaching, and the people that I serve at my church have been blessed. So I went there that night with a great sense of joy and affirmation of her ministry.

The passage that I lifted as a basis for the preaching is an Old Testament passage, but its prophetic truth transcends testament and context. It runs throughout all of life. It's found in the book of Isaiah, in the fortieth chapter, the fourth verse.

"Every valley shall be exalted, and every mountain and hill shall be made low: and the crooked shall be made straight, and the rough places plain: And the glory of the Lord shall be revealed" (KJV).

I want to talk about false vision, what faith sees. Faith sees what unfaith cannot see. Faith beholds what other entities cannot behold.

W. Franklyn Richardson is Senior Pastor of Grace Baptist Church in Mt. Vernon, New York and General Secretary of the National Baptist Convention, USA, Inc.

Note: This message was preached at the installation service for Prathia Hall Wynn at United Theological Seminary in Dayton, Ohio.

Even if one did not know the context of this prophecy, this text would be beautiful all by itself. It is metaphorically brilliant. If one just snatched it out of the poetry of the Old Testament, it would stand by itself. But when one hears the context of the passage, it takes on still richer meaning.

These are a homeless people who had been displaced from Jerusalem; they've been away so long that they think they will never get home. They have made themselves satisfied in their despair and pressure. It's a dismal context. They're cut off from what they were, and they're trying to make do with what is. They are psychologically and spiritually removed from their homeland. Just geographically, they are a long way from where they want to be.

But this prophet stands up in the midst of this dismal context and makes this sweeping pronouncement that has seemingly very little visible or existential authority. It's almost as though he disregards reality; it's almost as though he doesn't even realize what the people are going through. Does he know what's going on? He stands up in the midst of this despair and says, "Every valley shall be exalted, and every mountain . . . ."

Looking at it literally, you would think that he was anxious to get home. Of course, he is, because there are many mountains and lots of valleys and crooked places and rough places that separate where he is and where he wants to be. But he's talking about more than that. I can tell you that the prophecy here is transcendent of this context. It's a cross-testamental notion; it's the same thing that Jesus talks about when he says that the last shall be first and the first shall be last. It's the same thing that Luther writes when he says that Jesus reads Isaiah until the Spirit of the Lord is upon him. He is not tripping out; he has the authority of his faith. He stands up and with faith defies context.

Now the context in which we live, here and now, is dismal. People are destroying and wasting their potential. Addiction to crack and cocaine is common in the streets of our cities; the context in which we live is a dismal context. For the last several years, a hoodless Klan has worked to turn back the gains that we and our forefathers and foremothers have died to accomplish.

Fortunately, the preacher does not get his word or her word from the existential context; the preacher gets the word from somewhere else. Because the local context is often so very discouraging, we would go around with nothing at all to preach or sing about, unless our faith did defy our context.

Our forefathers and foremothers were sensitive people who understood this. You permit me to preach in the current context of my ethnicity, and I might bring severe suspicion of my closest associates of other ethnic groups. But I am dissuaded by the faith of our forebears which defied their context, and most of them simply refused to be embittered.

We can see for ourselves that somehow they had faith that defied context; they stirred the remainders of tribal religion and selected Bible text in a pot of faith. And in the midst of a dismal context you will hear them singing "I'm so glad trouble don't last always."

Faith defies context. And any woman, especially a black woman, who is shackled with this duality of oppression, racism and sexism, any woman who stands up and decides on her own to accept the call of God to preach must have such faith! So the context of the prophecy is relevant to oppression, but so is the content. Listen to what the prophet says, not only to the context in which he says it, but to what he says.

He says that the mountains and the valleys are in tension with one another; the mountains and the valleys are in conflict with one another. When one looks at South Africa, that's what Mandela's release is all about. The valleys and the mountains are in tension with one another and the valleys are someday going to rise, and the mountains won't hold them down. The rough places will have to be smoothed and the crooked will have to be straightened. It's happening in East and West Germany; it's happening all over the world, that the mountains and the valleys are in tension with one another.

When one looks at Ethiopia and other starving nations, many are dying while we just sit here. It is not because God does not give enough food to this world. It is because some folk have too much and some folk don't have enough. The mountains and the valleys are in tension with one another. The prophet in a dismal context wisely says the mountains shall be leveled down and the valleys shall be raised up. The rough places shall be smooth, and the crooked places will be straightened out, and the last shall be first, and the first shall be last. God is at work. Don't let what you see in the context limit your faith or your efforts.

That's the vision of creation, that's the Judeo-Christian vision, that in this world an era of justice and rightness is going to come. That's the hope that's in us. We can't justify it. We can't say how it's going to happen; it's just in us. It's faith, and faith defies context. The problem we have in the churches is that so many of us have no sense of vision. The function of this vision of faith is to instruct our actions until we arrive at our destinations. We ought to ask ourselves what would this world be like if God had God's way? I can tell you that when God has God's way, the mountain shall be made low and the rough places shall be made smooth, and the crooked, well that'll be made straight. The prophet said God is going to have God's way.

But then, when we do have vision, it is often parochial. It's *my* family, *my* church, *my* people, *my* denomination, *my* sex. It's always selfish and narrow. But it seems to me that God has an interrelated world, a global family and we know all that. The truth of the matter is that everything today is tied together. The luxury of America's wealthy is not unrelated to what happens in South Africa. There is no way to say that what happens to white people anywhere will not affect black people, and vice versa. What happens to black people will affect white people sooner or later, one way or the other. Everything is related.

What happens in one part of the world affects us all. America robs and rapes underdeveloped countries of their natural resources, and those countries turn into drug-producing economies in order to survive. And so drugs are produced in Colombia, smuggled into Panama, and our boys and girls buy them on the streets of New York, Dayton, and Los Angeles. Everything is related.

The prophet says every mountain and every hill shall be made low. You know, I'm excited about what God has already done in this regard. I'm excited about the *wasness* of God. I'm excited about how God stepped out into the absence of anything, to launch a beginning of the cosmos, and out of that nothing, made everything. I'm excited about how God flung the stars amidst the darkness, scooped out the valleys, and raised up these same mountains. I'm excited about that.

I'm excited about what God has already done—how God has directed the larger contours of the course of history, even though we are left to be free moral agents. That's what the Bible is. The Old Testament is a constant reminder of how God reaches out and delivers us and seeks to save us. I'm excited about how God came in Jesus in a back street of Bethlehem to teach and minister to us, and how he died and took the sting from death, and snatched the victory from the grave. Oh yes, I'm excited about the wasness of God.

I'm excited about the *isness* of God—about what God is doing right now in this time, in this location. I'm excited about God's isness in the ordination of women, which represents a movement of history that has great potential. I sense a place of service for God's hand-maidens that will be rewarding, fulfilling, and deeply satisfying.

But you know, I'm most excited about the *shallness* of God, what God will do. Most of us who are not making it off the isness or wasness are making it on the shallness. That's how slaves made it. Our slave ancestors didn't get encouragement from the was or the is.

I had the privilege to ask, "Please, Mr. Mandela, tell me. Was there ever a time in that twenty-seven years that you ever thought you would simply starve and die in prison?" He said, "No, because hope never dies." He was caught up in the shallness. For twenty-seven years he lived in a discouraging isness. But after a while isness is always overcome by the shallness of God. It's what some from the old school called "living in the not-yet while in the already." This is the already with a sense of the not-yets. Oh glory, the shallness of God.

That's what the prophet says. That's where you've got to live, my dear sisters. That's where you and all of us who are participating in the works of God have got to live, even when the isness is so much better than what it was. That's what the prophet says with great hope. Listen to him. He says, "Every valley shall be exalted, and every mountain and hill shall be made low: and the crooked shall be made straight, and the rough places plain." Israel shall return home, some slaves shall be freed, but there are still swords to be beaten into plowshares and hungry to be fed, whole nations and classes and genders of folks to be liberated. There are many valleys yet to be exalted.

In the New Testament it's the same thing; now are we the sons and daughters of God, but it does not yet appear what we *shall* be. But he shall appear, and we shall be like him, for we shall see him as he is. And I stand in awe of what God will do when God's clergy team is enriched and strengthened by more and more people like our sisters here and everywhere.

WHOM GOD CHOOSES, GOD USES

ELLA PEARSON MITCHELL

TEXT: I Corinthians 1:26

It's a great honor to be asked to preach the gospel at such a time as this. This evening we are gathered to witness one of the most historic occasions taking place in an equally historic church—a church whose current significance lives up to its remarkable history. This church is under the pastoral leadership of one who has been used of God to break down some walls of partition and prove in the laboratory of life, what is that good and acceptable and perfect will of God. I need not beat around the bush. Across the family of black Baptists today is a prevailing issue—I might say a *raging* controversy—with a variety of answers. Succinctly summed up, it might be: Whom does God choose for the preaching of the gospel? Just how does God go about selecting those who are to bring the precedent-shattering Good News?

Let us look at a passage seldom seen as an answer to today's inquiring mind; yet, it offers a most comprehensive response: First Corinthians 1:25-31. Was Paul overstating it? Or was it just *Corinth?* According to the way the established system selects or screens for intelligence now, not many wise, not the smart ones—a few but not many—not many mighty, not many noble ones are called. What kind of movement is this? How could the Corinthians ever influence world history?

Ella P. Mitchell is Visiting Professor of Homiletics at the Interdenominational Theological Center in Atlanta, Georgia, and editor of both volumes of *Those Preaching Women*.

Note: This message was preached at the ordination of Martha Simmons at Third Baptist Church in San Francisco, California.

Well, the Corinthians were not the first strange choices according to the world's systems. To be sure, there was a nobleman named Isaiah, but many more of the Amos type. Ezekiel was a priest, but hear Micah's words used for the theme of the 1960s revolution: "To do justly, and to love mercy, and to walk humbly with thy God" (Micah 6:8, KJV). Esther was a serious mistake according to the system that chose her. Nobody in the system knew how Deborah got to be a judge and a general. They give Huldah's credentials through her husband, but not as a competent person in her own right. Yet, her wisdom was the final word on the holy Scriptures found in the temple ruins. Questionable? We won't even mention how the disciples were called!

Apparently, God does not pay any attention to the way we determine whom should be called to preach or serve, and God never has. Socially speaking, there was very little status to the people Jesus called to service. Even among the disciples, there were several crude, cursing fishermen, a despised tax collector, and as questionable a character as Judas turned out to be. Some of the women who helped Jesus were certainly not in the top of the line. He befriended publicans and sinners during his ministry.

Are you ready to agree with Paul? Why on earth do you suppose Paul was saying all that he tells the Corinthians? Surely you realize that Paul was writing to his most difficult, one might even say, to his *most troublesome* church, the First Church at Corinth, where trouble was always abrewing. You see, Paul was defending himself against the charges that very possibly were being made by the Apollos bunch. They were holding out that Paul's preaching was too simple, too unsophisticated. In a word, they were calling Paul, of all people, *ignorant.* Paul could very well have called to remembrance his academic and ecclesiastical credentials. But he starts out this time in a totally different mode, setting forth some principles almost never clearly spelled out and examined. This amounts to the undoing of the "in crowd." The title "wise" always equals the wisdom of the crowd in *power,* that is by definition. Whatever we who hold the reins find wise is decreed by our own authority to be the wisdom of the time. And of course, in our gut, "in crowd" wisdom, we are not anxious to change anything. When we are in charge and in power, we are not about to shift that which would reduce our standing. This is true throughout human experience.

The music of America has been enriched not from the top, but from the bottom. The real creativity in American music is not nearly so close to European classicism as to the plaintive and sometimes joyous strains of an enslaved people.

The church, my beloved, is no different from the rest of civilization; it is not renewed from the top either. Today as one watches the tremendous decline in church membership, one is bound to expect that the greatest hope for reviving America's pulpit lies in the tradition of the black church.

Henry and I are in possession of a number of written requests for persons to teach preaching in our seminaries. And retirement is long past for the two of us. Invariably, we have received those requests because there is abroad in the land an awareness that the African American preaching tradition may very well be God's provision for the renewal of the church, a provision manifestly established by simple folks, the ones from the bottom. The books we write today name only the best of a tradition that is more than two hundred years old.

But the black church itself needs renewal. With all the potential—all the amazing possibilities—resident in the best of the African American churches, the truth is that most of that church is loafing along in anything from mediocrity on down the scale. We are often using a powerful tradition just to keep the doors open and to achieve some selfish ends. I am certain that the African American church must itself be renewed from its own bottom, from its own supposedly less wise, from its own weakest sources, from those on whom it has too long looked down—*women!*

So we have an insight that this, then, may be God's pattern. God chooses not many wise, not many noble, not many powerful! For that which is most likely to renew a church or a civilization is most likely to come from the bottom.

Beloved, this brings us to a second profound insight—God chooses the weak for reasons within themselves and not just by default of the powerful. God takes those who are least respected, often put down, those who are least honored, those considered least wise, oftimes because they are more receptive. Their minds and their hearts are open. They are willing and indeed anxious to please their Lord, because they know what it's like at the bottom. They have nothing to lose.

We teach in our homiletics classes against roll calls, but I can't resist one right here. I recall God's choice of a man named David, the least impressive of Jesse's five boys; I think of God's choice of Peter, an unlearned, profane fisherman whose works in the Bible were dictated to the more learned or more trained Silas or Sylvanes. (No, Peter couldn't write and I suppose he couldn't read, either.) Recall the women at the tomb who were given the great assignment to tell the Good News of that all-important event, the resurrection. The record names some of them, but the others were so near the bottom as to be obscure and nameless. But on them fell this eternal honor!

As I let the echoes of my mind go back to the last eight classes that earned the M. Div. at the School of Theology at V.U.U., I remembered that six of the eight valedictorians were women, and that in spite of the fact that the S.T.V.U. female enrollment is small, under the average. It may even be less than 5 percent. Presently, as I watch the students with whom we teach preaching at I.T.C., time after time the best understanding of the insights taught from the preachers of old is by today's generation of gifted women.

We are gathered here this night to ordain a woman—a woman whose grasp of the subtleties of the best of our tradition is among the most accurate. She won the preaching prize at Emory's Candler School of Theology last year. Here was an African American sister with that endowment. My beloved, the establishment may not be ready, but God is! And our God is not a respecter of persons, our God is a good God. I've said it before and I'll say today, "Sisters, preach on. God will provide all your needs."

Our text says to all those who are outside the circles of power, whatever group or whatever culture, whatever social status—the least, the underdog, the persons of low estate, the ones at the bottom of earth's junk pile, the unsophisticated, the powerless—whom God chooses, God uses. God doesn't delegate God's assignments to a committee. God does the choosing as only God can.

No committee would have set Presca (of the Priscilla and Aquila team professors of homiletics and theology) apart to teach theology to the fledgling Apollos, but God didn't need a committee or anybody to make the choice of that gifted woman.

What committee would have selected a chubby girl converted in Charleston, South Carolina, in 1925 to be a kind of entering wedge for the breaking of the barrier against women? In high school, God called her attention, but she had heard from reliable sources like her own mother that women were not supposed to preach. Strangely enough, her preacher-father never said a discouraging word to her.

In college she halfheartedly changed her major to religion in her senior year. Later when she served as an S.S. missionary in rural South Carolina, she would still not admit to preaching.

That woman continued to resist a call to preach even after seminary preparation, teaching in seminaries, and through the years delivering the "Word." Then one Sunday morning fifty years after her first word from the Lord, the Holy Ghost just snatched her out of the pew. She went running down the aisle to tearfully confess her "call to preach." God insisted and the Holy Spirit moved to the *ordination*. God be praised! God had chosen her, and God does move in mysterious yet powerful ways.

Not many wise, not many powerful, not many recognized in the established church are chosen. Not many that a pulpit committee would pick, not many that a local church would give a unanimous call with rights and privileges. But God's thoughts are not our thoughts and God's ways are not our ways. God's choices are not our choices. And I'm glad about that. God is not about to waste half of God's gifts and talents because they are not used in the male-dominated tradition.

Not many wise, nor many important, not many recognized are chosen, but whoever, whenever, wherever, or however God chooses, God uses! God is beyond our prediction and God will surely use this sister and other sisters to respond to that unique call this day and any day. Glory, Glory, Glory! Glory be to God!

"COME, SEE . . . SHE SAID"

ANTHONY C. CAMPBELL

TEXT: John 4:1-42

Read the fourth chapter of John, verses 1-42, from a "red letter edition" of the New Testament. If you only read the black print, a startling thing happens: the clear voice of a woman, petulant, angry, argumentative, clever, and full of guile comes through. Read it in light of the risk to the life and work of Jesus, the risk Jesus took in speaking with her under any circumstances. Finally, notice with care the outcome of the interaction between Jesus and the woman. You may conclude that truly Jesus is no respecter of persons, and that all the preaching in the story is done as testimony—the testimony of the nameless sister who preached her initial sermon and was called by God through Jesus to preach at least this one great sermon!

Jesus was in the middle of a crisis in his ministry. Nothing else could explain the fact that he put himself and his followers in jeopardy by going via Samaria to get to his old preaching ground in Galilee. The Pharisees regarded his ministry as more dangerous than John the Baptizer's. The word was out that Jesus was baptizing more than John. Those of us who debate over the approved formula of baptism (amount of water, correct explanation, and appropriate words to say) should take note: Jesus baptized no one and left no correct method. But Jesus, to get back to Galilee (and here the King James Version gives the proper urgency), "must needs go through Samaria."

There were ancient and deep wounds between the Samaritans and

Anthony C. Campbell is Professor of Homiletics and Preacher in Residence at Boston University School of Theology.

43

Jews. During the years of hostage taking, when the better classes of
Israel and Judah were in secure and none-too-uncomfortable exile in
the suburbs of Babylon, the remaining common folk had developed
religious practices that the detainees, upon their return, did not agree
with. There had always been syncretism between Canaanite cults
and the Hebrew tribes. Children were sacrificed, semen and blood
were taken to guarantee the status quo, and idols, totems, and magic
in high places were worshiped. These practices persisted through the
Judges, Prophets, and Monarchy even to the divided kingdom. The
loss of Jerusalem, first to a rival dynasty, then to the sword by
invaders, called forth renewed interest in the practices of Canaan.
Fusion of some sort with elements of the conquerors' religions and
culture also occurred. It was not simply the issue of intermarriage, for
this practice was commonplace. Those in Babylon were equally
guilty, but the Samaritans were singled out for harsh words and
harsher treatment by Ezra and Nehemiah, leaders of the returnees.
Matters were made worse when the Samaritans and their allies actually sabotaged the rebuilding of Jerusalem's walls. Even stronger
feelings arose when the returned "nabobs and snobs" declared all
Samaritans to be members of a mongrel group, blasphemers and
apostates. The acrimony became so great that all kinds of curses,
invectives, and prohibitions were mutually used. We have few
equivalents, in our time, to the hate and blood feud between these
groups over generations.

The Jews felt that these Samaritans had moved the ritual fires that
announced the feast days, confusing the orthodox. Pilgrims going up
to Jerusalem were routinely robbed or taxed or beaten, so the story
went. A few years before Jesus came, someone put human bones on
the High Altar in Jerusalem and defiled the place. The Talmud,
Torah, Hoft Torah, and Midrash all cited reasons to avoid the
Samaritans, their water, food and cooking utensils, even their shadows!

How amazing that Jesus could, on numerous occasions in preaching, take these outcasts, these unredeemable blasphemers, wrong-
headed, wrong-hearted, and despised, and use them as examples of
right conduct and as fertile grounds for the preaching of the Word.
Jesus, knowing the danger, *had to go through Samaria.* John, especially,
paints the picture of the subtle but pervasive hopelessness of the
preaching situation of Jesus in Samaria, and the risk that Jesus took

in speaking where, when, and to whom he did.

First of all he was alone, an impoverished rabbi on the run; single, lacking in utensils, in the wrong place talking to the wrong person. No unmarried rabbi could be seen with an unescorted single female. (And to make it worse, the Pharisees routinely thanked God for not having been made a Gentile, a dog, or a woman.)

Second, this was not just a woman, this was a Samaritan woman, unmarried, unchaperoned at her well! With Jesus' ministry already under pressure, he was in the wrong place at the wrong time with the wrong person, and without witnesses to his intention.

Finally the evidence is clear that this was no ordinary housewife or maiden lady (as my grandmother used to say), but someone very special. She did not go to the town well in Sychar, but went to the well outside of her city. Not only was it the roadside well, she went at midday to do the chores. Those who know rural life will note that no one gets the daily water at noon, unless she can't go where the decent folks go in the morning. These clues suggest that Jesus ought to have left the site immediately, for he was about to be contaminated—the single rabbi with the Samaritan woman of questionable reputation. John points out the hopeless picture of someone outside of the possibility of help. John always gives the *sitz im liben** in such a way as to illustrate the danger, the opportunity, and the lack of remedy except through God's good work, persistent purpose, and loving search for humankind. The rabbi and the hussy confront one another.

If you read the Scripture aloud, and read only the woman's words (not any of the words of Jesus), her sarcasm and incredulity leap off the page. This is an unattributed story of the drama of a saved soul that John the Gospel-Teller knew. There are no other witnesses to the transaction. It must be *her* story, and like much of the oral tradition, written and made canonical by the early community of faith; all knew the subject of these incidents, and no names for blind, crippled, helpless, or hopeless needed to be given. We eavesdrop on the testimony of one of the saints and the story burns with each telling.

At the outset, the Samaritan sister answers Jesus with a simple statement that no Jew has dealings with a Samaritan. She knew his Jewishness not by introduction but by the way he was dressed. He

*German: "setting in life."

wore the fringed outer garment of the confirmed and regularized
Jewish male. Those who have expended energy and argument about
wearing pants in church have misread Leviticus. The men's clothing
that a woman must not wear is this identifying tasseled three-piece
outfit the Jew wore. The Samaritan woman knew Jesus' credentials
before he said a word.

The Sister of Samaria now spells out some of the theological and
conceptual impossibility that Jesus is under. Not only must there be
no dealings between the two of them, but Jesus can't possibly deliver
on the promise of new, special water, for he has no cup, he has no
dipper, he has no access to the only well she can see. And it is deep.
Jacob had prepared this well, and it had supplied his family; Jacob's
cattle and progeny had all used this well. This lone rabbi with neither
kith nor kin, with no servants and no equipment, can't deliver on
anything, not for this woman, not at this well, and not in this land.

Jesus' next argument is less persuasive than his former argument,
and her derision now drips with unbelief. "The data are clear. You
have nothing, Rabbi, but if you give me this water, I'll take it, for if
my thirst is sated forever, I won't have to drink, fetch, get, seek, need,
or carry water ever again. Give me this water," she says, to silence
Jesus.

At this point the level of impossibility builds higher and higher:
a Samaritan, a woman, a town party girl, hussy, tramp; and an unmarried rabbi, no tools, no retainers, and no willing ear to hear his
sermon of salvation. The stiff, neglected Samaritans are causing Jesus
to risk the kingdom of God and its proclamation to the House of
Israel by talking to this hopeless and hapless person. But now the
radical shift occurs. The generalized thrust of the story of Jew and
Samaritan is replaced by preacher and subject, savior and sinner,
hope-giver and hope-needer.

"Get your husband!" Common-law, wife-in-law, shacking-up
candidate, borrowed mate. "Who are you in relationship?" No longer
is the woman argumentative, but now she must testify as to who she
really is. Her language is careful; now she is unsure of the way the
question is leading. Is it a trick to get her stoned, a way of making
her a candidate for banishment? "I have no husband." She is careful
and clever. (It's like asking your son, "Did you drive my car?" and
his answer is, "Not today!" But if you ask, "Have you driven the car
without my permission at anytime?" you get a simple "Yeah!")

"I do not have a husband, I have no husband, I have no relationship like that, or, would you repeat the question?" In that moment,
evangelism is possible, preaching is called for, movement is discernible: Jew, Gentile, Samaritan, man, woman, all become one. Jesus now
establishes an affirmative action program for all people. No historic
barriers to separate us; no east, west, black, white, good, bad, Samaritan, Jew, Gentile; just need and gift.

"You have had a bunch of conjugal relationships. You have played
wife to five persons. You are the jaded, the fallen, the needy in the
midst of your questioning my authority and sincerity." Jesus seems
to be winning. But he is really calling out of tombs, out of trees, out
of separation.

One more time the woman shifts the venue. "You are recruiting
for your mountain. You Jews feel we have no authority in Mount
Gerizim; you always felt our worship site is wrong so our ritual is
invalid. You want us to come to your mountain, Mount Zion."

But Jesus still moves toward his "call" of this woman of the streets
of clay to streets of gold, from messing around to Messiah ground.
Not real estate but real religion, not mountains but the maker of
mountains. "We Jews have a charge to keep," says Jesus, "but we
children of God will someday glorify God apart from a mountain."
Jesus has dodged all arguments, to raise the level of dialogue above
water, cups, Jews or Samaritans.

The reaction to this exchange is the focus of the authority and the
authentication of the call. Some have said that if God had wanted
women to preach, Jesus would have had women among the twelve
apostles. Don't hedge God. Jesus had no Gentile apostles, no black
apostles, no English-speaking apostles. The Holy Spirit after Pentecost (the Jewish graduation day) opened the door at Cornelius' house
to the Gentiles, the birthday of the Gentile church (Acts 10).

Jesus took the despised, soiled, rejected, outcast and sent her running with a message. *Evangelion* is the running, *kerygma* is the message,
and as soon as *she* told somebody, *she* was preaching. Evangelism: the
message and the preaching, the messenger, the message and the telling; that woman got called to preach that day. Her text was simple:
"Come, see a man." Her delivery was simple: "He told me everything
I ever did." Her result was electrifying: all, all, all rushed to see what
had altered the town floozie and made her the herald of Good News.

One day while traveling back from a funeral in California, I attempted to use a "super saver" airline ticket. I was informed I could not alter the terms of my reservation. I had to stay until Saturday (it was Friday), and I could not change the arrangements I had made. My insistence drew a crowd. I got loud; the woman behind the counter got quiet. I called for a manager; none came. Then I got pitiful and got sympathy, but no change. But the day supervisor called me down to her counter. I went down with fear and trembling, for she was black and appeared to know how to say no to black men. She whispered to me that she knew who I was, that my mother had taught her in Detroit, that my father had helped her get the job, and that she was in charge of the ninety persons who wrote tickets. She took my useless ticket and tried to reconcile the fare, but the computer rejected her efforts. When the computer screen started to blink, she entered her code for authorization and then pressed "CE" on the keyboard. My curiosity was aroused, and I asked her what she had done. She said that the computer program could not allow the ticketed fare to be used, but a window in the program allowed a supervisor with the authority and access code to override the old program and give a new set of instructions, if the situation merited. She said after she gave her authorization she cancelled my old reservation by pressing "Cancel entry" and then put in my new reservation. Handing me my boarding pass, she said, "Get on board!"

One day on Calvary's ragged brow Jesus authorized that my old reservation be changed, overriding my old plans. "CE" became "Christ Eternal," and authorized a change by accessing my life. The old reservation I'd made was invalidated and my boarding pass, like the Samaritan woman's, was reauthorized and reissued, and we all got on board.

Jesus called her; Jesus called me. Jesus called the woman with the issue of blood, Jesus called Zaccheas, Jesus called the first church meeting together in the upper room, men and women together about 120 in number, Jesus sent those women from the tomb preaching the Good News, Jesus can, does, will, and has called!

"Come, see a man!" She preached!

alone in the hot sun toting a jar of water. "Give me this water,"
I told him emphatically, "that I may not thirst, nor come here
to draw."

I prepared myself to receive this water; yet what he said next
did not have anything to do with water. "Go, call your husband
and come here," he said in a manner that I really cannot explain
but which led me to respond openly and honestly. "I have no
husband," I told him.

His response shocked me and showed me that indeed there
was far more to him than meets the eye. "You are right," he
said, "in saying, 'I have no husband'; for you have had five
husbands, and he whom you now have is not your husband;
this you said truly." I was astonished by his revelation. He had
never seen or heard of me before and yet he knew all about me.
I looked into his eyes and sensed that he knew how I had given
up, resigning myself to a life that is always beginning and
ending. As I looked upon him again, I reflected on how, knowing all about me, he had dared to talk with me, ask a drink of
water of me, and offer me a spring of water welling up to eternal
life.

Suddenly my soul began to glorify the Eternal One because
I knew that this was someone with whom I could open up,
someone with whom I could talk. My people, do you know how
I have longed to talk with someone about the eternal? Yet living
in a culture such as ours—one bound by stringent tradition and
law—I could never question or talk about our religious institution aloud. That is why I dared not waste this opportunity that
the Eternal One had put before me. I began to talk straightaway
about things that you say women dare not discuss. "I perceive
that you are a prophet," I told him. "Our ancestors," I continued, "worshiped on this mountain; but you Jews say that in
Jerusalem is the place where people ought to worship."

His response was even more startling than his revelation
about my lifestyle. He said, "Woman, believe me, the hour is
coming when neither on this mountain nor in Jerusalem will
you worship God. You worship what you do not know; we
worship what we know, for salvation is of the Jews. But the
hour is coming and now is, when the true worshipers will

worship God in spirit and truth, for such are those whom God seeks as worshipers. God is spirit, and those who worship God must worship in spirit and truth." Those were his exact words. My people, he said that we do not know what we worship and that indeed the Jews do, because salvation is from them.

I know that the Jews have this Messianic claim, which they believe to be a promise from God. The prophets prophesied about him. He is to be their anointed king. And although we do not believe in all of those latter-day prophets, we are nevertheless looking for the restorer, the true teacher who will be a prophet in the stature of Moses. But what he did was explain the difference between our emphasis on the law of Moses and the Jews' revelation that came by way of the prophets.

His next statement went beyond even Jewish claims. He said that God is spirit. If that be the case, God cannot be limited or defined by tradition and custom in man-made sanctuaries like our Mount Gerizim and their Jerusalem. If I understood him correctly, what he was saying was that God the Eternal Parent transcends class, race, place, and time. God moves freely, touching however, whenever and wherever God chooses. Moreover, God wants true worshipers—people, you and I—worshiping without restraint in spirit and truth; that is, by God's power, in God's will, and by way of God's revelation. This is indeed good news for us.

My next words flowed instinctively from my mouth. "I know that Messiah, the one who is called Christ, is coming, who having come, will show us all things." When I said this, his face appeared to glow and he spoke words that left me speechless. "I who speak to you am that very one," he said. I was forced to ask myself, "Can this be the Christ?" I again reflected on our conversation: He had offered me living water, revealed my past and present, said that God is spirit and that "the hour is coming and now is when the true worshipers will worship God in spirit and truth." His words were full of promise, anticipation, and fulfillment. It was as if he were saying that the gift of God was being realized in my presence through him.

I was anxious to converse with him further. However, some men showed up and I could tell that they were astonished at

seeing the two of us talking. Yet, they did not say anything, and
so I left my water jar for him and started home. I must confess
that I did not plan to tell you or anyone about my experience.
But something within would not allow me to waste this God-
given opportunity. I could not keep it to myself—*I had to tell
somebody!* That is why I must ask you again, my people, "Can
this be the Christ?" I beseech you, come see for yourself.

After telling my story, I still did not know if the crowd would
come with me. With facial expressions that ranged from disbelief to
astonishment, they had remained silent as I shared my good news.
However, I had to move forward regardless of whether they followed
me or not. And so I began to press through the crowd and head in
the direction of the well. Do you know what happened? My people
followed me! They followed me to see the Christ!

Every time I recall that afternoon and what followed my eyes '
overflow with tears of joy and my soul leaps with gladness. Who, I
ask you, would have believed that the Eternal One would choose
me—a Samaritan woman, a rejected and despised earthen vessel—to
be among the few to whom the Christ first revealed himself, to be
among the first to proclaim the Good News, and to be the first to take
the Word outside of the circle of the Jews? Yes, the Eternal One
enabled me to meet the Christ at the dry and thirsty wells of my life.
But that is not all, my people; when I met the Christ, I received water
that was not from the well and I could not keep it to myself—*I had
to tell somebody* because

> I heard the voice of Jesus say
>   "Come unto Me and rest;
> Lay down, thou weary one, lay down
>   Thy head upon my breast!"
> I came . . . as I was, [rejected,
>   and despised], weary, and worn, and sad;
> [But in the Christ, I found] a resting place,
>   [and now I am truly glad].
>
> [But that is not all, because] I heard [the Christ]
>   say, "Behold, I freely give
> The living water; thirsty one,
>   Stoop down, and drink, and live!"

I [stooped] . . ., and I drank
Of that life-giving
    stream;
My thirst was quenched, my soul revived,
And now [right now,] I live in [Jesus the Christ!
Jesus the savior of whomsoever-will].[1]

---

[1]Adapted from the hymn, "I Heard the Voice of Jesus Say," by Horatius Bonar.

A THIRST FOR THE KINGDOM

BARBARA HARRIS

TEXT: John 4:5-26

We have in this passage from the fourth chapter of John's Gospel an interesting story that begins with a little verbal sparring match between our Lord and this woman who has come to draw water from the well of Jacob. As we try to put this encounter into some focus and some context, I ask you to think with me on the subject "A Thirst for the Kingdom."

As I reflected on this passage of Scripture, with its detailed encounter between Jesus and the Samaritan woman, I was mindful of the fact that on Women's Day we usually hold up as examples women of unquestioned character, unblemished reputation, and solid achievement. And certainly many quickly come to mind, not only from the pages of Scripture but from everyday life as well. We tend to focus on the virtues of womanhood and, again, almost everyone here could extol these. Moreover, on Women's Day we tend to highlight strengths rather than weaknesses, fine points rather than faults, and sterling qualities rather than sins. We usually hold up the "perfect," but in this text we learn from the "imperfect."

Jesus, on his way from Judea to Galilee, is passing through Samaria. He is passing through unfriendly territory. The rivalry between Jews and Samaritans was well known; it had existed from the time of Esra and Nehemiah. Jews and Samaritans had serious theological differences. Jews didn't think much of Samaritans, for they had profaned the sacred altars of the Jews by letting pigs run loose through the temple. In fact, to the Jews, Samaritans were not only

---

Barbara Harris is Bishop of the Boston Diocese of the Episcopal Church.

unclean, they were barbaric. That is why the disciples and others were shocked when Jesus used the parable of the Good Samaritan to illustrate his answer to the question: "Who is my neighbor?"

They also were caught up short by the story of the cleansing of the ten lepers, the only one of whom returned to give thanks was a Samaritan. The Jews could not imagine that Jesus would use a Samaritan as a good example of anything.

So it is odd that, although weary from his journey and the midday heat, our Lord would stop to rest in this hostile place. Most of us would try to get through hostile territory and on to familiar or neutral, if not safe, ground as quickly as possible. But our Lord, as on so many occasions in his ministry, chooses an odd place to stop and to witness to the glory and love of God. And he stops in the odd places of our lives.

It was not unusual, however, that Jesus—who often broke with tradition—would request water, even from a stranger, a member of an enemy group, a woman. Water was life-sustaining in that parched and barren land. His disciples, we are told, had gone off to buy food. But even though one could survive without food, one could not go for long without water. And his request was one that would not be denied, even from a sworn enemy. Life was much more simple in that time; there were just certain things you did not deny people. Scripture was very clear on hospitality to strangers. So Jesus says to this woman with her water jar, "Give me a drink."

But our Lord is after more than just water. Jesus, resting at this physical fork in the road between Judea and Galilee, in the course of his journey to his ultimate earthly destination, Jerusalem and Calvary, also is at a spiritual crossroads. His mission is coming full cycle as he makes his tortuous journey that culminates in our salvation. And he is about to do something he has not done before. Here he reveals to this woman of the hated Samaritans, this woman of questionable repute, something he has refrained from revealing to others who might be regarded as more worthy of his attention. Jesus reveals to this woman in no uncertain terms that he is the *Messiah*.

There have been other instances up to this point in which the Father's glory has been shown through the Son and in which he carefully has told others that it was not yet time to lay out the full story. At the wedding feast at Cana he told his mother his hour had not yet come; on the Mount of Transfiguration, where caught up between Moses and Elijah he shone forth in radiant beauty, he cautioned his disciples to tell no one of what they had been privileged to see. He gave similar admonishments in some of his miracles of healing. Yet here at this crossroads, he makes himself known to this woman.

As if to further document his revelation, he goes on to tell this woman about herself. He blows her cover as if to reinforce the truth that before God the secrets of all hearts shall be revealed.

It shocks us when somebody sees through us and discovers what we would rather keep hidden. We go to great lengths to try to cover up our secrets. We make sure we are seen with the right people in the right places; we join the proper organizations and institutions, including the church. You can fool your friends, but you can't fool Jesus!

It is human nature to try to cover up the unflattering, the unattractive, the uncomfortable things about our lives. At first, the woman at the well tried to be cagey. She tried to dodge the question and the issue. "Go and get your husband," Jesus instructs her. "Sir," she says, "I have no husband." "Right," says Jesus and proceeds to detail her liaisons and her indiscretions. "You've had five husbands and the man you have now is not your husband." Imagine our reaction if personally confronted that way by Jesus today: "Now look here, Jesus, you done left off preaching and gone to meddling!"

She also challenges him when he says, "If you knew who you were talking to and what God is offering you, you would be the one asking 'give me a drink.' And he would give you living water." "Are you greater than our father Jacob who gave us this well?" she asks.

But Jesus stays right on the case. "Everyone who drinks of this water will thirst again, but whosoever drinks of the water I shall give will never thirst."

Ultimately this woman realizes that she is conversing with someone different, someone special, somebody with something to offer, someone who could make a difference in her life. And that's what Jesus is all about—making a difference in our lives, helping us to emerge into our full stature as children of God.

I think there are some clear messages for us in this strange story of the woman at the well: messages for us as we stand at our individual and personal crossroads and ponder the choices of life in a vain world that is no friend to grace; messages as we consider ourselves emerging people of Christ's kingdom; messages for us when we realize, as did the woman at the well, that while we are not yet what we should be, thank God we are not what we were. We are different because God has touched our lives, different because we realize we can learn from all of God's people, even from folk like the Samaritan woman—a street woman if you will.

No matter what you think of the Samaritan woman, a fact—and an important fact—is *that she was at the well.* She was there where Jesus was. Had she not gone to the well when she did, she would not have been privileged to meet and to have an encounter with the Savior.

No matter her reason for going at the odd hour she went (and scholars tell us she didn't go at the usual time, at the early dawn or in the cool of the evening). She went in the burning heat of the day when the sun was scorching, when everybody else was looking for some shade, for some relief from the midday heat. No matter her reason for going at that hour. She was at the right place at the right time. If you don't go near the well, you cannot draw up water. You must make yourself present and available to receive the living water God so freely gives. You must go to the well!

Too many people are absent from the well. Because the woman came, she received a blessing. Simply because she came, she received a blessing. So many stay away and do not avail themselves of the blessings that can be theirs.

People stay away for various reasons. Some feel like the Samaritan woman, scorned and derided because they lead different kinds of lives. Others feel rejected because of who and what they are. Some stay away because they don't want to rub shoulders with those they consider undesirable, those who don't fit in for one reason or another, those who are poor or shabby.

Some get so locked up in their own troubles, their own trials and tribulations, so trapped in that small box of self-pity, they are absent from the well. Some are so caught up in the pastimes and pleasures of this world, they absent themselves from the well. They sing, "Go, Spirit, go Thy way, some more convenient day, on Thee I'll call."[1] Some are so puffed up with self-righteousness, they don't even think they need a drink.

People are absent from the well not realizing Jesus can give them

---

[1] From the hymn "Almost Persuaded," by Philip P. Bliss.

a new heart, a new mind, a new song to sing, a new way of looking at life, a new way of loving other people—even the unlovable—if they have a thirst for the kingdom.

Another fact to remember is that *the Samaritan woman brought a vessel.* If you have not come up in the country or visited a rural area where folks rely on wells, you might not know about drawing water. Getting water from a well is not like cupping your hands or holding a glass under a faucet or pressing a button on a water fountain. If you are going to make use of a well, you must bring something with which to draw water. The woman told Jesus, "Sir, you have nothing to draw with and the well is deep."

That is true of God's grace. Too many of us come to the well empty-handed. We bring no vessel in which to draw up the living water.

People say, "I come to church, but I don't get anything out of it." If you don't bring anything in which or with which to get something, then you *won't* get anything. We bring to the throne of grace the thin shells of ourselves instead of open, trusting hearts and souls, vessels in which to draw up the living water. If you don't bring something, you can't get anything. If you don't believe God can do something for you, you'll never know when or what God does.

Lastly, the Samaritan woman not only received a blessing, *she went and told others.* "Come see a man who told me all that I ever did." Come see for yourself. The woman at the well became a well woman and shared her wholeness with others.

Too many of us do not share what has been given to us. If we would witness to what we have received, others might come and receive also. When is the last time you told somebody what the Lord has done for you? When is the last time you shared with someone that he brought you "a mighty long way."

My friends, we thirst after many things in this world. We thirst after money, power, prestige, position. We put our trust in them, we even pray about them. But like our Lord, we too are at a crossroads, in the church and in society. We still have a choice and the question our Lord is asking us is "Do you have a thirst for the kingdom?"

Jesus is asking us "Are you content to settle for the temporary thirst quenchers of life: the material values of this world, the right connections, the proper credentials, the things on which this society places so much value, things that will never slake the thirst of your parched, dry souls? Or do you thirst after righteousness, after peace, after justice, after the liberation for all of God's people?"

Do we thirst after those things that make for a just society as Jesus proclaimed his Father's kingdom to be? If we gave our testimony this morning would we sing with the psalmist, "As a hart longs for flowing streams, so longs my soul for thee, O God"? (Psalm 42:1) Seek ye first the kingdom of God and his righteousness and all things will be added unto you.

Do we have a thirst for the living water with which God truly enriches our lives? Do we have a thirst for the kingdom? Do we have thirst to truly emerge as faithful Christians to be more than we are?

Each of us must answer for herself or himself: Do we have a thirst for the kingdom? Jesus is patiently waiting for our answer.

SURPRISE:
GUESS WHO'S
COMING TO THE PULPIT?

J. ALFRED SMITH, SR.

TEXT: Luke 24:10

When the gospel of the Risen Christ was first told, the experienced preachers with seminary credentials were mute. Peter, James, and John, the star pupils of three years of seminary training with the Master Teacher were surprised. The redemptive word of the first fruit of them that slept was not theirs to proclaim.

These men who had studied the doctrine of redemption with the Redeemer had no living word for bereaved and broken hearts. These men, who had an inside track on the revelation of the supremacy of grace over the Law and the prophets, were the sole witnesses to Jesus communing on the Mount of Transfiguration with Moses, the law-giver, and Elijah, the peerless prophet. But this precious message of the foundation of our faith was given to others.

Surprised? You should not be. The last became first. Those women, who were the last at the cross, were the first at the empty tomb. As Moffatt translated it, "Some women of our number gave us a surprise" (Luke 24:22).

The surprises of God came to us through the surprises of the women. How surprised were the preachers of macho theology! They were surprised by God with the theology of the womb.

The first surprise of God came to us in the genealogy of Jesus Christ as recorded in the Gospel according to Matthew. Macho theologians of orthodox Jewish thought would begin their day by thank-

---

J. Alfred Smith, Sr., is Senior Pastor of the Allen Temple Baptist Church in Oakland, California. He is the former president of the Progressive National Baptist Convention, Inc., and Visiting Professor of Homiletics at several San Francisco Bay area seminaries.

ing God that they were not born Samaritans or women. A macho theologian lists Tamar, Rahab, Bathsheba, and Ruth, as the only women included in our Lord's family tree. Tamar gave birth to twin sons by tricking Judah, her father-in-law, into going to bed with her. Rahab was the prostitute who helped the people of God to conquer Jericho. Ruth, a native of Moab, an enemy nation, became the grandmother of King David. Bathsheba, the wife of Uriah, gave birth to Solomon, David's son. Four women were used by God to teach us the power of grace to transform human lives, so that they can be used for God's own glory.

As if we are, according to Williams's translation of Luke 24:25, "sluggish in mind and slow in heart to believe," God found it necessary to surprise us again by bestowing grace upon a peasant girl. Her name was Mary, "and the angel said unto her, Fear not, Mary: for thou hast found favour with God" (Luke 1:30, KJV; the New English Bible translates it, "for God has been gracious to you"). Mary was not yet the wife of any man. She was a virgin who gave birth to the Lord without the sexual intimacy of a husband. Isn't God filled with surprises? Can't we men see that the Sovereign God does not need us to accomplish God's will? God's use of male clergy is an act of grace.

And now there is the biggest surprise of all. "It was Mary Magdalene, and Joanna, and Mary the mother of James, and other women that were with them, which told these things unto the apostles." Mary Magdalene had a stained past. Joanna was the well-off wife of a government official. Her husband worked for Herod. Joanna could have been a society belle. But she made Jesus her choice.

There were other women. These anonymous women were ordinary women. They were women like my mother. They were women like your sister, your aunt, your cousin. Think of other women who were tutored by Jesus. There is the Sunday school teacher who toiled prayerfully to teach you about God's love. There is that choir director who taught you to sing, "Yes, Jesus Loves Me."

There are yet other women who cook for our church suppers, usher for us at our church services, sing for us before we preach, and tell us that we have preached great sermons when we know that we have failed. And there are still other women who set the Communion table and then wash up the Communion trays and glasses, so that we can justify ourselves with our macho theology as we serve the Lord's Supper to other sinners saved by grace.

Thank God, brothers, that there have always been other women who served the Lord while we were fishing, or frozen with unbelief— women like Sojourner Truth, Harriet Tubman, Mary Church Terrell, Mary McLeod Bethune, Dorothy Height, Marian Wright Edelman, Ella Mitchell, Prathia Wynn, Renita Weems, Malvina Stephens, Myrtle Griffin, and Brenda Cooper.

Doctor W. A. Jones, pastor of Bethany Baptist Church of Brooklyn, New York, said that if the faithful sisters left Bethany en masse, the following Sunday he would stand in his pulpit and say farewell. Yet so many of us are surprised at the surprises of God. How defensive we are when some of these women tell us that God has called them into a preaching ministry. Whereas Moffatt translates Luke 24:22 as "Some women of our number gave us a surprise," too many of us behave with the response indicated by J. B. Phillips, who translates the same passage as follows: "and some of our womenfolk have disturbed us profoundly."

What did the women say that was disturbing? Did they preach the Law? No! Did they preach wisdom literature? No! Did they preach the humanism of the proverbs or the existentialism of Ecclesiastes? No! They preached no didactics. They preached no apocalyptic opiate as some of us do. They did not have more sound than sense, majoring in "the whoop" in an attempt to massage the emotions of the hearers. They were not Sunday morning entertainers. They were not preaching a prosperity gospel. They preached the truth. Jesus is alive. He is risen. Death is dead. Jesus has kept his promise. Believe the gospel.

These women walked humbly with Jesus. They never troubled Jesus about seats of status for themselves. They were content to be servants. They were given the revelation and the message because they were faithful. They knew the joy of service. They knew the fellowship of being in the presence of Jesus. They were following Jesus for what they could give and not for what they could get. Hence to them were given the words of the Kerygma.

But now, brothers, the disciples did not believe the resurrection gospel of the women. If these brothers could trust women to nourish them in infancy, to provide security for their childhood fears, and to marry them and rear their children, why could they not believe their Good News story? If Jesus could trust women with the gospel of his resurrection, why didn't the disciples trust them? Why don't we trust women who say they are called to preach?

Give to our sisters the courteous hearing that our sisters give to us. Women of the cloth must tell their story. No male orator can tell it with the flavor of feminine insight. Let them alone to tell us how Jesus brought them through the long agony of lonely nights and the aching anxiety of endless days. Let them tell how the risen Christ forged their suffering into alloys of pure gold. Let them tell how Jesus helped them assume so-called masculine responsibilities while maintaining feminine sensibilities. Let them tell how they wept at blood-soaked Calvaries and marched through the interim of waiting upon the Lord.

Yes, they waited. They waited patiently. They waited until they could see on Sunday morning a resurrection of the angelic over the demonic. Let them preach. They have their own story to tell. Not even angelic tongues of heavenly messengers can describe the mystery of how Jesus changed their names from "wenches" to girls, from girls to Aunt Janes, from Aunt Janes to servants of God. Not even the women of Galilee or the daughters of Judah could speak more eloquently of the magic mystery, marvelous majesty, and matchless mercy of the grace of God.

SURPRISE PARTY!

JEREMIAH A. WRIGHT, JR.

TEXTS: Mark 16:9-11, Luke 24:8-11, Luke 24:22a

"Some of the women of our group surprise us!"

Both Mark and Luke describe a situation that has not changed much in almost two thousand years. God surprises the church by what God shows to a woman! Jesus reveals himself as the *Risen* Lord to a woman! He tells her, corroborates John, to go tell the *men* what God has done, what God is doing, what the Lord has said to her, and how the Lord has commissioned her. And when she obeys the Lord, the church doesn't believe her! (Luke says the church doesn't believe *them*—none of the women!) Both Mark and Luke describe a situation that has not changed much in almost two thousand years.

God still surprises the church as it approaches the twenty-first century. God still surprises the church by what God shows to *women.* Jesus reveals himself as the Risen Lord . . . to *women!* Jesus calls them by name! Jesus tells them to go present themselves to the men as persons who have been sent by the Living Lord. He gives them direct orders to go tell the church what God is doing, what the Lord wants them to do, what the Lord wants the church to do, what the Lord has said to them, how the Lord has commissioned them, how the Lord has spoken to them, how the Lord has sent them; and when they obey the Lord, the church does not believe them! "Some of the women of our group . . . surprise us!"

Now I have maintained for quite some time that one of the reasons

Jeremiah A. Wright, Jr., is Senior Pastor of the Trinity United Church of Christ in Chicago, Illinois. He received his D.Min. from United Theological Seminary in Dayton, Ohio.

the church did not, and does not, want to hear such a radical message is because of the problems we have with the *messengers!* They are women; and we have all been programmed to believe that women have their place; and that they need to stay in their place!

We have women astronauts, and women chemists, women sprinters and women singers, women judges and women architects. We have women on the basketball court and women in the Supreme Court. We have one black woman who plays with the Harlem Globetrotters and another black "fine" woman who can outrun most men! We have women mayors, women governors, women as chiefs of police, women as city managers, women firefighters, women police officers, women in the armed forces, and women in Congress!

Yet? . . . We put limits on God when it comes to women in the pulpit. Now, lest you think I'm talking about you and not me, let me tell you how deeply ingrained this cultural brainwashing is.

About a year ago, I was on my way from Los Angeles to Chicago, and after the airplane taxied out to the active runway, the flight attendant went through her routine about seat belts and emergency exits; she reminded us to make sure all seat backs and table trays were in their appointed and locked positions. Then as we turned onto the runway to start our roll in this great big DC10, this other *woman's* voice came on saying: "Good morning, ladies and gentlemen. This is Captain Wilkerson and we are next for take-off. So, flight attendants, take your seats and I'll get back to you when we are airborne!" . . . and I tried to die! I almost screamed out loud, "Who's going to fly this big bird?"

I, who had no problems with a woman in the pulpit, got right nervous about a woman in the cockpit! All of us are culturally conditioned about this issue of women "being in" or "staying in" their place!

One of the reasons the church did not, and does not, want to hear the message that the Lord of the church gives them is because of the problems that we have with the *messengers.*

In the book of Joel, quoted by the apostle Peter in his powerful sermon on Pentecost, the Lord says,

> "Afterward I will pour out my spirit on *everyone:*
> your sons and *daughters* will proclaim my message;
> your old men will have dreams,

and your young men will see visions.
At that time I will pour out my spirit
even on servants,
both men and women."
(Joel 2:28-29 GNB; italics ours)

Stop putting the teachings of culture into the mouth of Christ! God said God was going to have women preachers, so who do you think you are to say we are not going to have women preachers? When did you start voting *out* of order what God has already decreed as divine order?

The church did not and still does not want to hear the message that the Lord gives women because the church has a problem with women! But let us please be clear that that is *our* problem. That is *not* God's problem! So let's stop trying to put God's stamp of approval on the mess we are making of God's ministry! The women couldn't get a hearing because they were women!

To my sisters in ministry and to my daughter in the ministry especially, here is the word for you from this passage! Don't let what the church does change *you!* These women did not change their mission. They went where the Lord sent them anyhow. These women did not change their message. They said what he told them to say anyhow; and these women did not change the *messengers!*

Just like we can't sit still and watch black folk try to "out-white" white folk, you don't change who you are because of where you are; and you don't change what you are, based on what folk like or dislike! If God has called you to the pastorate, God has called you *as* a woman! Don't change the messenger!

God gave you a message about a Risen Lord who is able, a Risen Lord who confronts every system of evil with all power in his hand, a Risen Lord who will be a battle-ax, a wheel in the middle of a wheel, a strong tower of defense, bread when you are hungry and water when you are thirsty! God gave you a message about a man named Jesus who can change lives and change hearts, change situations and change habits. Don't change the message! Don't change the messenger and don't change the message!

God gave you a mission that the church wasn't ready for then, and in some places the church is still not ready for it; but don't change the mission! Preach what he tells you to preach! Preach when it feels so good it can't "get no gooder"! Preach when you don't feel like preaching! Preach when men and women believe you and preach when they *don't* believe you! Don't change the mission! Preach when they receive you and preach when they don't receive you! Don't change the mission!

Remember: God is throwing a surprise party, and *you* are just extending an invitation to come to God's party! God is full of surprises. God always has been, and God always will be! When it was time to redeem humankind, God took the symbol of the lowest, the most undesirable specimen in the eyes of men and said, "Surprise! I can use what you look down upon and get me a Savior and *man* won't have anything to do with it but be an observer and a recipient! Maybe then you will understand that what I think of women and what you think of women are at opposite ends of the spectrum!" When it came time to send the boldest message ever heard—"He is risen from the dead"—God took that same symbol and elevated her to the position of the first apostle saying: "Surprise! What you consider important and what I consider important are two different things altogether! The ones whom you exalt and those whom I exalt are selected by two different sets of criteria!"

Now, my sisters in the ministry, Mary and the other women messengers were able to be obedient and faithful to God's magnificent mandate, not changing the messenger, the message, or the mission; and I submit to you that they were able to be obedient because they did what I am recommending to you.

Mark gives us one clue in his description of Mary. John gives us another clue in his description of the resurrection scene.

Mary remembered where she came from. She remembered what the Lord had done for her. He claimed her and he cleansed her. Don't ever forget what the Lord has done for you! Mary remembered who it was that called her ("Mary!"). If you ever hear the Lord's voice, don't ever let anybody make you doubt what you heard from on high! Don't ever forget who it is that has called you! And then, Mary remembered not only where she came from, who claimed her and cleansed and who called her; but she also remembered who kept her! She knew not only where she came from, but she knew where she was going!

This ministry God has given you, this message God has given you, this mission God has given you, the surprise party that God is throwing is not only for a city called Columbus or wherever it is you are called to serve, my sister. It is not only for a city called Chicago or a city called Baltimore. It is also for a city called heaven! Remember where you are going!

And the best way to remember is to thank him (like Mary!) every chance you get. When you get up in the morning, thank him! When you come into your office, thank him! When you walk into the church building, thank him! When you walk into counseling situations, thank him! When you walk into a crisis situation, thank him! For every new member that comes because God is using you as a vessel to preach the gospel, thank the Lord Jesus! For those of you in the pastorate, when you preach and nobody joins, just for the opportunity to preach the gospel and for God's audacious trust in us earthen vessels, thank him. Thank the Lord! For all that the Lord has done, thank Him!

If the Lord has ever delivered you from something—as he delivered Mary of Magdala—then you know what it means to have something to thank God for! If the Lord has ever done something for you (as he did for Mary) then you know how Mary felt, and you know what it is like to get up in the morning thanking the Lord, to go to bed at night thanking the Lord, to go through every day thanking the Lord, and to live a life that is bathed in a prayer of thanksgiving!

What you are doing, in effect, is reversing the negative prayer of a curse that was prayed by the rabbis and putting that prayer in its proper perspective. They thanked God that they were not born women. You thank God for making you as you are, and for choosing you as you are; and remember the words of the apostle Paul: Just be obedient "unto the heavenly vision!" (Acts 26:19). God bless you, sisters. Keep on preaching!

WHAT MAKES YOU SO STRONG?

VASHTI M. MCKENZIE

TEXT: Judges 4:4-5

In the Old Testament Book of Judges we find a strong woman by the name of Deborah. And perhaps if we can look at the things that made her strong, we might uncover the answer to our own questions of strength.

Deborah is a "bad" sister. And she is part of a great company of women found in the Word of God. There is the wisdom of the prophetess Miriam, the devotion of Naomi, and the love of Ruth. There is also the persistence of Hannah and the astuteness of Rahab and the late-in-life blessing of Sarah. And now we come to the prophetess, Deborah.

Israel's form of government was a loose confederation of twelve tribes. There was no king, although the people would ask for one later on. The judges were the ruling authority under God.

Israel continued on her spiritual seesaw. She lived up and down in her relationship with God. That's a lot like us, up and down in our faith. One day we're following Jesus and the next day we're leaning upon our own understanding. One day we're in the church and the next day we're out. We live like hell Monday through Friday and then try to make heaven our home on Sunday.

The Old Testament is very clear. Follow God and you will be blessed. Turn away from God and you will receive curses and the judgment of God.

So, after the death of Ehud, Israel blew it again. God's chosen

Vashti M. McKenzie is Pastor of the Payne Memorial A.M.E. Church in Baltimore, Maryland, and is National Chaplain for Delta Sigma Theta Sorority, Inc.

71

nation went whoring after other gods. As if they needed more gods. They had the one true God. The Lord of Lords had extended merciful kindness towards them. They were children of the promise fulfilled and the land had rest for eighty years. Who could ask for anything more?

Yet, we who are children of the promise fulfilled in this generation still go looking for other gods. We make gods out of money, power, prestige, employment, and possessions.

When the people of Israel turned their backs on God, God forsook them. God let them be oppressed by their enemies. They became slaves to Jabin, the king of Canaan, for twenty years. Israel cried unto the Lord, for Jabin was a mighty king and the captain of his host was a mighty warrior. Sisera had nine hundred chariots of iron.

Now, you and I may not be impressed by nine hundred chariots, but to the nomadic people, who were used to camels, tents, and desert sands, nine hundred chariots of iron were tantamount to a nuclear weapon.

The writer in the Book of Judges notes that Deborah, wife of Lapidoth, sat under the palm tree and Israel came to her for judgment.

It has been said upon several occasions that during this time in history, Hebrew men rose every morning and prayed the same prayer. They prayed and thanked God that they were not born women. So, all of Israel came to the very one that they prayed they didn't want to be like. They came to a woman for the administration of justice. They came to a woman to settle disputes, disagreements, and arguments. They came for interpretation; they came for answers; and if they wanted to know what was on God's mind, what was the latest Word from heaven or what was God's will, they came to her judgment seat, perhaps in the open air under the shadow of a tree that bore her name.

The sister was bad!

She was not elected by popular vote; she was not appointed by a governor, mayor, council member, or president. She was not voted in by a majority in an electoral college; she was not nominated by the Israel senate. Deborah was assigned by God. No "if, ands, or buts." She judged with the authority of a prophetess, called and empowered to be God's mouthpiece to Israel during the oppression of Jabin.

One day, as the story goes, Deborah sent for Barak, the son of Abinoam out of Kedesh, Naphtali. She asked him, had not God commanded him saying, "Take an army of ten thousand and go over the river." Didn't God say, "I will deliver Sisera and all his chariots into your hands?" Can you imagine that confrontation between Deborah and Barak? Barak probably had the same feelings we have when we are confronted with something that we think that no one else knows about, or when someone confronts us with a truth we have denied.

Deborah said, "Didn't God tell you to do something? Didn't God say, 'I will back you up'?" Hasn't God ever told you to do something—take on a responsibility, teach, go and serve, pull together a family, begin a job, work on a relationship, or lead a parade? And for one reason or the other, you somehow allowed the truth of God's command to slip between your fingers. Just watch! God will send somebody to remind you, just like Deborah reminded Barak.

Barak said, "Well, I'll be happy to follow God's instructions. But I won't go unless you go onto the field of battle with me." Deborah replied, "But understand that God will give you the victory, but the honor and glory of the deliverance from Sisera will ultimately go to a woman."

So Deborah and Barak went to war, facing the enemies of God, moving out on God's plan of deliverance. And all of the enemies of God were defeated. The victory won, Deborah and Barak sang a song of praise to the glory of God. Deborah judged Israel forty years and God gave her rest.

Now, what shall we say of these things? What made Deborah so strong?

The first thing we can see is that she had a job and did it!

She was assigned, called, and set aside by God as a prophetess and a judge. The execution of her job was not dependent upon whether other women were called to do the same job. The effectiveness of her ministry was not dependent upon whether other prophets agreed with God's selection. The shouldering of her responsibilities was not dependent upon public opinion of the community or religious leaders of the day. Her being a prophetess and a judge was not dependent upon the whims and fancies of her society, but upon the call of God.

There is strength in knowing your job and doing it.

The second thing we can see is that she must have had a balanced work and family life. After all, Deborah was a wife working outside of the home.

She was the wife of Lapidoth. To be childless during this period of history was a disruptive negative in the life of any wife. Since her barrenness is not mentioned, she was perhaps a mother as well.

In any case, when the time came for her to go to war, there is nowhere recorded that her husband or her children gave her any flack. She went to war. And she had to have had it all together, for she doesn't say, "Barak I'll go with you, but first I must get permission from my husband. . . . I'll go, but first let me put another load in the washer. . . . I'll go, let me see if I can get a sitter for a few days."

And yet Deborah had to come out from under that tree sometime. She had to let Lapidoth know that she loved him, how important he was in her life.

There is strength in developing a balanced work and family life.

The third thing we can see is that she knew how to work in relationship with other people.

Getting the job done required a group effort. Deborah knew how to give God's instructions and get support. She knew how to lead without ostracizing other leaders. She knew how to gain a consensus and motivate towards a common goal. Deborah had enough sense to develop good people skills. She worked with Barak, not on Barak. She worked on God's agenda and not her own.

There is strength in working together.

The next thing we see is that she did it all in love.

By her manner and conversation, we know that Deborah did it all in love. You have to love someone to be able to resist saying, "I told you so," or "What took you so long?" She loved Barak enough not to berate, belittle, humiliate, castrate, lay him low or lay him out. And we must do the same with each other.

There is strength in loving others.

And finally, Deborah had a God connection. I mean she didn't just climb under that palm tree on her own. She didn't carry that responsibility because it was a nice thing to do. But she must have had an alive, abiding relationship with God. So that when God called, she answered. She must have had fellowship and communion with God. She must have had a consistent prayer life to make her requests known to God, for Deborah's faith took her from the palm tree to the battlefield and on to victory.

There is strength in a relationship with God.

What makes you so strong? You find strength in knowing your job and doing it, in balancing work and family life in working in relationship with others, in loving others, and in having a relationship with God.

May you always find the strength. Amen.

WOMEN FOR SUCH A TIME AS THIS

MARTHA JEAN SIMMONS

TEXT: Esther 4:14

God has not said that the only persons who could be or would be called to do a job for God would be the educated, the wealthy, the descendants of royalty, the strikingly attractive, or the old and wise. God requires only that those who do the will of God be willing to submit to the ways of God no matter what.

Centuries ago in the country of Persia, in a city called Susa, lived a king by the name of Ahasuerus. His queen was Esther. As far as historians can tell, she was from among the Jews who had been deported as slaves by King Nebuchadnezzar of Babylon. She was reared by a man named Mordecai who historians suggest was her uncle. Mordecai, although also a captive, had found favor with the king and was serving in a high official capacity.

Mordecai was a court officer and Esther was the queen. The sun was shining brightly for these two Jewish captives, and all the dark clouds seemed to have taken a noticeable vacation. But when Mordecai and Esther reached the top, it didn't mean that they didn't have some problems lurking in the shadows. In fact, being at the top meant that problems could be even larger, simply because they *were* at the top. One day, as Mordecai and Esther were basking in their accomplishments, bad news came. A man by the name of Haman, who was the king's vizier, his highest ranking official, had developed a dislike for Mordecai. You see, Mordecai didn't bow and fall prostrate when

Martha Jean Simmons is on the Ministerial Staff of the Third Baptist Church in San Francisco. She received her M.Div. from Candler School of Theology, Emory University, Atlanta, and in 1989 she was the recipient of the Candler Prophetic Preaching Award.

Haman came around, although everyone else did. This didn't set well with Haman. It was a blow to his ego. It made him look bad in front of everyone else. So Haman, who was an egomaniac, decided that he would go to see the king to have something done about it.

When Haman got the king's ear, the conversation went something like this: "O King, your majesty, I know you're busy, but as your second-in-command, I feel that I must bring to your attention an important matter. Your Majesty, you know that Persia has one hundred twenty-seven provinces, and they're filled with all kinds of people from everywhere. If we let one group get away with breaking the law, then other groups are likely to start thinking that they can do the same thing. Eventually you could lose the throne or even be put to death.

"Your Majesty, there is just one group that is acting up and getting beside themselves right now—only one group that is not following our laws. Now of course, if we make an example of them, then none of the other groups will have the nerve to get out of line. O King, just to show you how concerned I am about this, I will personally contribute a large sum of money to the war chest to help deal with this problem. I have worked out all of the other details. I've even set a date."

"Well, do as you will with these people," said King Ahasuerus. "Here, take my signet ring and use it to show that I've given my royal approval."

The king's secretaries were summoned and Haman dictated an edict of extermination that was to go to all the governors in the provinces. Copies of the edict were sealed by the king's ring and made official. The governmental gears went into motion and the decree was dispatched to the provinces in their own language. In that instant all the Jews in Persia were suddenly under a sentence of death! The national announcement that went forth said, in essence, "To all governors of Persia: Be it hereby decreed that because of their unwillingness to follow our laws, because of their general insolence toward government officials, and because they are a threat to our national security, all Jews shall be destroyed, including their women and children, on the thirteenth day of the twelfth month of this year. This will insure that our country will continue to enjoy peace and we will remain the strong, united country that we are. Be it decreed this day, by order of King Ahasuerus, Royal Leader of Persia."

The word spread quickly. Esther didn't get a complete understanding of what had happened, because she was in the king's palace, isolated from the people. All she knew was that Jews were mourning, weeping, and all upset. So she sent a messenger by the name of Hathach to see her uncle Mordecai to find out what was going on. Mordecai sent back the following message: "Dear Esther, our people are faced with extinction because of one maniac, who is also the king's second-in-command. You must go before the king and intercede on behalf of our people. Esther, you have the king's ear, and he must be made to understand that this just can't happen! Let me know what you're going to do. Urgent! Love, Mordecai."

When Esther got the message from Mordecai, she sent him her reply: "Dear Uncle Mordecai, I received your note and I'm sorry to say that this is not as simple as you think. I may be the queen, but my role is not highly valued. I haven't even seen the king in thirty days, and I'm the queen; can I make it any plainer than that? Also, Uncle Mordecai, to show you how powerless I am I'll tell you that anyone—even the queen—who goes before the king without being summoned by him, is supposed to be put to death. And I mean anyone, including me. He could kill me and replace me just as easily as he replaced his last wife. So, Uncle Mordecai, please understand. I'd like to help you, but I can't. I don't want to see our people perish, but my hands are tied. I know that this is a cruel and awful thing to have happen, but there's really nothing I can do. This is such a major problem that it is out of my reach. I am just a woman, with no real power. I hope you understand. You remain in my prayers."

Esther, unwilling to take a risk, claimed that she was powerless, but Mordecai knew better because God had already spoken to him in a dream. So he sent Esther another letter. "Dear Esther, I got your reply and you need to know that you can't just cry that you are powerless and pray and that's it. You have to use your position to do something, no matter how risky. And if you refuse to do something, don't think that because you're the queen your name won't find its way onto the extermination list. Remember you are still a Jew, too. Also, God can save our people, and not spare you because you won't stand up. You've said yourself that the king could easily replace you with someone else. Esther, you don't have to speak to the king on our behalf. But think about it. Who knows? Perhaps you've come to the throne for such a time as this. Your becoming queen wasn't just a stroke of luck or an accident. And now that you have been elevated, do you not understand what your responsibility is to your people? In hope, Mordecai."

That did it. Esther didn't need for the message to be any more clear. Queen or no queen, palace or no palace, royal robes and diadems or not, she could not forget her oppression and that of her people. The letter from Mordecai stirred up something way down deep in her soul. She replied immediately. "Dear Uncle Mordecai, I got the message. You call the people together and you all fast and go down in prayer for me. I'll do the same and then I'll go see the king. Uncle, I know you're right. I realize that unto whom much is given much is required. Were it not for others I wouldn't be sitting on the throne and enjoying a life of luxury. I was made queen for a reason. So, soon and very soon I'm going to see the king, and if I perish, I perish."

Esther fasted and prayed. Then she went to see the king. When she approached him, she fainted and had to be revived. As she began to speak, she almost fainted again. Finally, the king, now a bit impatient but still sympathetic, said, "Esther, why are you here? Tell me what's on your mind. Whatever it is that has you so troubled, tell me and I'll fix it. Whatever you want, tell me and I'll grant it. I'll even give you half of all my kingdom if that's what you want." Esther said, "King, I'd like to have a banquet. I'll tell you then what I want."

In the meantime, God began to move and do what only God could do. You see, when oppressed people find themselves in distress, it's not because God is dead. The people just need to rise up and do something for themselves and then God will do the rest. So, after Esther saw the king and put her plan into motion, then God went into motion. Late that night the king couldn't sleep. So he sent for his sleeping pill of last resort, a servant to read the court minutes. This would put anyone to sleep. The servant read and read. When he reached the part about an assassination plot that had been uncovered, the king sat up in the bed and cried, "Has that man Mordecai ever been properly rewarded for uncovering that plot and saving my life?" The servant replied that he had not.

The next day the king called in Haman and asked him how he should honor a man whom he wanted praised. Haman, thinking that the king meant him, suggested that the king go all out and spare no details. The king said, "Haman, that sounds good. Do everything that you said. Don't leave out a thing, and do it all for Mordecai."

Meanwhile, God kept moving. The time for the banquet arrived and Esther said, "O King, if I've found any favor in your heart, you'll rescind the decree that went out saying that all Jews were to be executed. O King, please spare my life and that of my people."

"Esther, who had the nerve to issue such a decree?"

"Your adversary, your enemy, Your Majesty—it was Haman."

The king was so upset he walked out of the room. Haman then begged and pleaded with Esther to have the king spare his life. The king came back and saw him lying in a compromising position before Esther and the king said, "I know you wouldn't dare violate the queen while I'm in the building." Then a busybody said, "You know, King, there is a hanging gallows already set up." The king said, "Hang him, hang him, hang him on that."

God didn't stop calling women to stand up, after Esther. One day, a cancer called slavery came. God peered from the balcony of heaven and said, "Come here, Sojourner Truth. I need you to stand up and speak out in such a time as this." Then things got worse and God said, "Harriet Tubman, I need you to organize an Underground Railroad, in such a time as this." God kept moving and one day, God said, "Rosa, I don't want you to give up your seat on the bus. I need you to set off a movement in such a time as this."

And God is still calling women to stand up. If God has given you something to do in such a time as this, do it—no matter what the risk—and leave the outcome up to God!

THREE WOMEN AND GOD

GARDNER C. TAYLOR

TEXT: The Book of Ruth

We almost always preach about men. A great deal is lost, I think, when we overlook a full half of the human family. And so, now, I want to preach about some women. I wanted to call this "A Family Love Story," but that does not quite say what I wish to say. And so I will call it "Three Women and God."

The book of Ruth is an intriguing book, sometimes said to have been written to establish a certain ethnic openness among the people of Israel. But it is also an endlessly engaging book. I always put the little blue thread right at the Book of Ruth, because I can never find it. It is set so early in the Old Testament that I am always looking somewhere else for it. The word God is mentioned very little in this book, and yet it is one of the noble expositions on what seminary people like to call theodicy—the ways of God with humankind.

It is the account of a family: Elimelech, his wife Naomi, and their two sons, Chilion and Mahlon. They migrate from Israel because hard times have come upon that land. They travel east of the Jordan to Moab, whose purple hills formed at evening an almost somber background to the long, strange history of ancient Israel. They have gone to Moab seeking a better life. All of us who are children of migrant communities might well ponder what must have gone through the minds of this man, his wife, and their two sons. We might especially wonder about the father and mother who are giving

---

Gardner C. Taylor is Pastor Emeritus of the Concord Baptist Church in Brooklyn, New York; former President of the Progressive National Baptist Convention, Inc.; and Visiting Professor of Homiletics at Colgate Rochester and Harvard Divinity Schools, and Union Theological Seminary, NYC.

up familiar surroundings and are about to make their way, to establish their home in a strange land. It is likely they knew very few
people in this land, where they would be looked upon as foreigners
among people whose customs were not familiar to them.

Some competent person ought to set down in a skillful way the
account of our black migrations in America, and the raw, ugly circumstances that prompted the migrations of blacks from the South,
northward and westward. These were a people driven by circumstances. How great must have been the anxiety they felt as they sat
for the last time by the lamplight of their humble Southern quarters.
These people were determined that their children would have better
opportunity than they had, and were willing to brave the hazards and
the uncertainties of what they had heard was a cold and hostile land.

When one looks back upon Naomi and her husband, Elimelech,
and their sons, one hears a replica of what many of us have gone
through. This was the pattern of migration for this family. They
establish a home. They make a life; and in the natural course of time,
the husband dies. These sons take wives to themselves. It is an
interesting thing to see romances take place, develop, blossom, and
flower. These lads, Mahlon and Chilion, marry Moabite girls, lovely
in their lithe, highland beauty. And for ten years, the two generations, this widowed mother-in-law and mother, these daughters-in-
law, and these two sons, all live together. But after a while, something occurs—and those of us who preach ought to never forget that
there lingers ever over human life an "after a while"—the two sons
die. Life is never one thing or the other. It is always a mixture of joy
and sorrow, of gladness and grief, of sunshine and shadows, of sick-
ness and health, of life and death. This is life, and preaching ought
never be far away from tears *and* laughter. Any preaching that is
going to search the hearts of people, must search them at the depths
of their gladness *and* at those profound moments of their grief. These
sons die because the generations rise and the generations pass away.

Now Naomi is left widowed. She says to her two daughters-in-
law, with a wonderfully mature beauty and character, "I have no
other sons for you and if I, barren as I am in my old age, could bear
children, you could not wait for them. Go back to your own people."
What unselfishness on her part. Some have suggested that maybe this
ought to be called the book of Naomi. There is a sense in which it
is she who is the heroine. She is willing to undertake whatever

uncertainties and hazards are involved in returning to her land minus her sons *and* her daughters-in-law. "Go back," she says. "Go back to your own people." They kiss. It is one of the unforgettable farewell scenes of Scripture. The widowed Naomi, now bereft also of her sons, starts back toward the land of Israel, having heard that circumstances have altered back at home. She says to her daughters-in-law, "Go back to your own people."

Orpah goes a few steps, kisses her mother-in-law, and turns back toward the hill country of Moab from which she has come. Perhaps Orpah finds happiness. Perhaps she marries again, for there is no beauty quite like that of a woman already attractive, who has known sorrow early in her years. And so very likely Orpah finds a new life, but for us she disappears forever. She has come very close to salvation history. One need not blame her; it is a natural impulse for her to go back home. But there is a certain sadness, a wee bit of melancholy, that settles upon us when we realize that here is a woman who touches so close to the whole lineage of God's revelation to people, and then turns away from it and disappears in the purple hills of Moab. How sad it is for anybody to miss life, but how doubly tragic it is for any person to come close to the meaning of life, to its richness, to its fullness, to its grandeur, to its glory, and to then turn away from it.

I spoke at Southern University and spent a day or two among the gentle people of my upbringing. I saw people there, hundreds of them, who have actually made it to places of great responsibility—people who came along in my time, who could not even go into a public library at one time. It can be done. But how tragic that a land like America, so blessed, so great, would now be so imperiled by a wicked liaison between greed and racism, so that the nation has penalized itself and paralyzed its energy.

And how sad that the heirs of the people who braved the uncertainties of migration, and who came out of the dark night of slavery with a bright vision of who they were and what they might become, should be succeeded in our day by so many who seem to have lost all sense of direction and purpose. I weep for the black American community when I remember whose descendants we are. I was born fifty years after slavery, or thereabouts. I've eaten in former slave quarters and preached in former slave churches, and I knew people who came out of that dark night. I knew their determination; I knew their courage; I knew their willingness to sacrifice. In 1854, the *Richmond Monitor,* which was then the leading paper of the city of Richmond, which would shortly be the capital of the Confederacy, printed an editorial, in which it said, "The Negro is here and is here forever. And he is ours and he is ours forever." In 1854, from the slave quarters of the South, there came a reply, not in the print of the *Richmond Monitor,* but driven out of heartbreak and hope, "I'm so glad trouble don't last always." How sad that we who are the heirs of that tradition should come now to a place where we do not know what is the next step we ought to take.

As the nation has chosen to turn away from its democratic vision by its choice of racism and sexism, so have we in our churches chosen to distort the vision of the kingdom of God by limiting the full exercise of the gifts of women. We have excluded women from the pulpit and other areas of church leadership and dared to claim that this is God's will. We are guilty of an unholy liaison between sexism and the privilege of power. This is not of God. There is in Christ neither Jew or Greek, neither bond or free, neither male nor female.

Ruth, with some deep interior motive of love and duty and regard for her elder, would not turn back. She speaks those tender words which are among the most romantic words, be they between boy and girl or between parent and child, in any literature in any part of the world. "Intreat me not," she said, "to leave thee, or to return from following after thee: for whither thou goest, I will go; and where thou lodgest, I will lodge . . . and thy God,"—had she seen this elderly woman in prayer?—"[will be] my God" (Ruth 1:16, KJV). Had she seen this woman's sterling faith under difficult circumstances? Had she found in her mother-in-law a role model? "Thy God will be my God." And let me say to you quite honestly, the strongest preaching that you will ever do will be in what you are. If you have principles and decency and purpose and a determination not to exploit your people, there will be people who will look to you and glorify the God of Heaven. The God of Heaven will honor your ministry far beyond what you will be able to scramble and scrounge and plot and scheme to receive. God will do it.

And so Ruth follows her mother-in-law. Boaz sees her and sees in her beauty, deepened by sorrow. Believe me, you're not ready to preach the gospel at its depths and heights until something has cut you. People can see a difference in those who have experienced pain.

They can tell when someone has not yet had that experience, too, as in the case of a young woman singing in a concert hall. A man in the the audience said to another, "There is something wrong with her voice." The other said, "No, there is not anything wrong with her voice; it is her soul. She has not been hurt yet." And some day, something will cross your life that will bring you to tears and heartbreak, but it will be the means by which you gain access to other people's hearts. And so Ruth enters the lineage of the household of faith.

When I turn to the fifth verse of that first chapter of the book of Matthew, there her name stands. She becomes the mother of Obed, Obed becomes the father of Jesse, Jesse becomes the father of David, and there in that lineage comes the Savior of the world. This Moabite girl, this alien child of the hills, this foreigner, this woman in a society that devalued and oppressed women, by loyalty to love and to duty, enters the covenant of grace. And her name stands there and will stand there as long as the stars shine and as long as the ocean moves, because she found that which is the most precious thing in the world, an association with the covenant of grace, in the household of faith.

Who could have imagined that God would choose to use a humble foreign woman in such a way? God's ways are not our ways. Yet some of us are trying even now to choose for God who should preach and who should not. Some have boldly declared, "God cannot call a woman to preach." How arrogant. How outrageous. The call by God to proclaim this gospel of light and life is completely in God's hands. It is a divine prerogative and only a divine prerogative. It is to our shame that we would miss the glorious gospel of Jesus Christ because we prefer our prejudices over God's choice of servants. We misrepresent our Lord and dishonor his name.

Years ago, I preached in a southern city where George Beverly Shea, the song leader for Dr. Billy Graham, was on the program that night. He told a story from his own youth, about his involvement in Wall Street finance, for which he had a real talent. It caused him to show up later and later for the customary family dinner and the gathering around the piano, as some of us did in the long ago, to sing the hymns of faith. His mother must have sensed that something was happening to him internally, so she left a note for him to come early from work the next day and to play a piece on the piano while the other family members were arriving for dinner. He said that she had left that simple, old, truly evangelical hymn,

> I'd rather have Jesus than silver or gold, I'd rather be His than have riches untold; I'd rather have Jesus than houses or lands. I'd rather be led by His nail-pierced hand. I'd rather have Jesus than men's applause, I'd rather be faithful to His dear cause; I'd rather have Jesus than worldwide fame, I'd rather be true to His holy name.[1]

I want to say to you something that I do not often say. I have come now to the evening of my life. It has been a wonderful day. I never dreamed, having been born when I was and where I was, ninety miles from where land runs out in the deepest South, that such wide opportunities should have opened to me.

However, let me say this to you from my heart, my young friends. The faith that I now have, I have not won in any bucolic cloistered surrounding. I have won my faith in the toughest arena in the world, in the unholy belly of public life in the city of New York. I've known people of great wealth, but I'd rather have Jesus than silver and gold; I'd rather have Jesus than riches untold. I have heard great auditoriums echo with acclaim from one end of the earth to the other. You name it—New York, Cleveland, Chicago, London, Tokyo, Miami— but I'd rather have Jesus than people's applause.

I have known great people, Malcolm, and Martin, and once, preaching in Old First Church about twenty-five years ago, I spent a morning with Albert Einstein. But I'd rather hear the gospel of Jesus Christ than all of the wisdom of scientific genius. No matter how famous or obscure the preacher, no matter whether highly educated or prayerfully self-taught, no matter whether male or female, I'd rather hear the riches of the pure and simple gospel than all of the astonishing insights of science. I'd rather have Jesus; I'd rather have Jesus than anything this world affords. I'd rather have Jesus.

---

[1] *I'd Rather Have Jesus* by Rhea F. Miller and George Beverly Shea. © 1922 and 1939 © renewed 1950 and 1966 by Chancel Music. Assigned to The Rodeheaver Co. (a div. of Word, Inc.). All rights reserved. International Copyright secured. Used by permission.

WOMEN TRANSFORMED BY CHRIST . . . FILLED WITH POWER

CYNTHIA L. HALE

TEXT: Luke 8:1-3

Jesus was making a systematic tour of Galilee traveling around the countryside preaching, teaching, healing, transforming lives, reaching the masses with the Good News of the kingdom. The twelve were with him, men whom Jesus had chosen to be his disciples during his earthly ministry and who would carry on the building of God's kingdom after his physical departure from them. Luke, the great physician, a man sensitive to and sensible about the place of women in the ministry of Jesus, records that among the disciples were certain women who had been cured of evil spirits and diseases.

Of the women who followed Jesus, only three are named. Mary Magdalene, Joanna (the wife of Chuza), and Susanna. Little is known about these three with the exception of Mary Magdalene. She is mentioned several times in the Gospels, often heading a list of women like her who had been transformed by Christ. This implies that she occupied a place of leadership in service rendered by women called by Christ.

Mary Magdalene is identified by her place of birth, Magdala, which was a prosperous trade center, located on the coast of Galilee, about three miles from Capernaum. She was a woman of high standing and comfortable circumstances, like the other women mentioned in this text. Not only does Luke link these women because of their status, but also because they had been healed of evil spirits and

---

Cynthia L. Hale is Pastor of the Ray of Hope Christian Church, Disciples of Christ, in Atlanta, Georgia. She received her D.Min. from United Theological Seminary in Dayton, Ohio.

infirmities by Jesus. Each of them no doubt had experienced physical, emotional, and mental anguish as demons possessed them, body, mind, and spirit.

Mary must have been the most severely afflicted, for Luke says that seven demons had come out of her. When Jesus first saw Mary she was, no doubt, obviously depressed, deranged, disoriented, afraid out of her mind, with no control of her life. But he could look beyond her confused state to the soul of a woman who would be a tremendous blessing to him and others. He cast the demons out of her. It is not recorded how he cured her or the other women. He really didn't have to do anything except be there. You see, there is healing and help in just his presence. But perhaps he touched her or called the demons out of her. Whatever the case, he healed her and transformed her into a whole person. Jesus liberated Mary from her darkness and oppression, just as he liberates us from the bondage of sin we find ourselves in, forgiving us, picking up the broken pieces of our lives, putting them back together again.

This is as far as most people go in the reading and comprehension of this text. For too many, it is simply another story of Jesus' healing or forgiving women who are typically named in the Scriptures as sick or in sin. But this is not just another healing or deliverance text. Actually, none of the stories of Jesus' dealing with women are. Read them again. For Mary, Joanna, Susanna, and the other women healed by Jesus, this was an empowering experience. Their healing was the manner in which he set them free to begin to take seriously their lives as women created in the image of God.

Transformed by Christ, these women no doubt began to see new possibilities for life and living. Transformed by Christ, they accepted his call upon their lives to engage in life and ministry with and for him.

They had debts of love to repay. Jesus had set them free not only from their physical and mental infirmities, but also from the societal restraints placed upon them. In surrendering their lives to Christ, they left their homes, the comfortable, the secure, to follow Jesus, and as Luke says, they used "their own resources to help." These women of Jesus' day were not typical women of their times performing typical tasks of women. This text suggests that women had a public and prominent part in the life and ministry of Jesus.

Jesus was not typical of his time either. Into a world where women were property and not persons, whose feelings and rights were of little concern, into a world where the "called" and the "chosen" were of the male gender, into a world where the woman's only place was in the home as a wife and a mother, came Jesus, born of a woman.

When God sent his Son, Jesus, to earth, he could have introduced him to the world in a countless number of ways. But Paul says in Galatians 4:4: "When the fullness of time had come, God sent his Son, born of a woman, born under the law."

Jesus loved his mother, cared and provided for her. Even from the cross, he met her need for comfort. He exalted motherhood, but he did not view women as capable only of being wives and mothers.

Jesus treated women as persons, as equals. He respected their intelligence, spirituality, and assertiveness. He resonated to their courage and faith. He was impressed with the Gentile woman's faith and forthrightness, thus he healed her daughter. He was honored by the woman with the issue of blood who courageously and boldly pressed through the crowd, just to touch the hem of his garment.

Jesus responded to, accepted, affirmed, and encouraged women. He defended their rights, by word and deed. He took issue with concepts and practices that viewed or treated them as second-class citizens. He felt for them in grief and illness. He brought their dead back to life, and straightened their bent-over bodies to allow them to stand up with dignity.

Jesus gave to women, and was open to receive from them. He took delight in their company and spent time in dialogue with them, revealing his divinity to them. He challenged them to develop their minds, abilities, and their gifts.

In the presence of Jesus, women are transformed and filled with power. This power enables women to break from the societal norms and expectations that prohibit them from living up to their highest potential. This power helps rid women of negative perceptions and images that cause them to feel inadequate and inferior. This power allows women to recognize within themselves feminine worth and value without having to take on the image of men or have men validate their existence.

Jesus, then, was about the task of infusing women with the spiritual strength and confidence of believing in themselves as equal children under God. Their dreams and aspirations were now not limited to traditional "women only" roles, but they had the power to determine their own destinies.

This is not the typical story of Jesus healing a group of women and sending them on their way to continue business as usual. No one who has had an encounter with Jesus can leave his presence and go back to business as usual. This is a story of God calling women into ministry, transforming and empowering them for the task. It is the story of women responding and giving of their gifts. Having received much, they gave much.

Sisters, this is our story. It is part of our rich spiritual heritage. Who are we? We are women transformed by Christ . . . filled with power. We are powerful, in control. We can handle anything. "No, we can't!" I hear some of you who are timid, unable to believe in yourselves, frustrated by having to prove your calling and your ability to preach, waiting for approval, needing to be affirmed. We struggle with the fear that comes to all of us—fear of inadequacy, fear of what others are thinking and saying, fear of not living up to the expectations of others, and fear of not living up to our own expectations.

"No, we can't!" *Yes, we can!* We can do all things through Christ who strengthens us, because he has filled us with his Spirit and with power. God has not given us the spirit of timidity or fear. He has given us a spirit of power and love and self-control. God has called us to live by faith. Live by faith and stir up the gift of God that is in you. The ministry requires boldness and courage that come from a confident faith.

Let go of your fears! Fear imprisons; faith liberates! Fear paralyzes; faith empowers! Fear discourages; faith encourages! Fear makes us useless; faith makes us serviceable! Fear puts hopelessness at the heart of life; faith gives us the courage to accept the call of God upon our lives to be faithful to God and to the will of God.

Mary, Joanna, Susanna, and the other women were faithful. They knew that the one who had called them was faithful. And as his servants, they followed Jesus from Galilee to Jerusalem. They were there in Pilate's hall, when Jesus was condemned. They were there that fateful Friday when he was nailed to the cross. They were there when he bowed his head and died. They were there when Joseph of Arimathea and Nicodemus laid him in the tomb.

Early that Sunday morning, these same women found the empty tomb; they went to tell his disciples. They were given the signal honor of preaching the Good News of the resurrection. Jesus lives! He lives in the hearts of all women and men, too!

A TALE OF TWO SISTERS

JEANETTE M. POLLARD

TEXTS: Luke 10:38-42; John 11-12:11

It's been almost three years since our friend Jesus' death, and people on their way to the Passover feast still stop through our town, just to see if I'm still around, and to ask the neighbors if the stories they've heard about my being dead and coming back to life are really true. It's kind of strange, the attention I get. But, because I know who the real heroes are, I quickly tell people that if it hadn't been for my two sisters, I wouldn't be around to tell my story.

Maybe you haven't heard of my two sisters, Mary and Martha. I'm not surprised. In our country not much attention is given to women. They aren't expected to be in the limelight, but are just to remain in the house and take care of household chores. It was really through my sisters that Jesus became our friend.

Our society says that men are better than women. That doesn't seem quite right to me. But, being in the minority, I dare not voice my opinion openly. That's why it helped to have Jesus come through Bethany from time to time. He made everyone feel welcome and showed no difference between males and females. My sisters just loved Jesus because he was one man who didn't try to fit them into a mold or tell them what was "proper" Jewish behavior. For my sake, I'm glad Mary and Martha didn't pay attention to that "proper behavior" rubbish, because, if they had, I wouldn't be here to talk about it today!

I have to tell you about my sisters' personalities so you'll get the

Jeanette M. Pollard is Associate Minister of the Messiah Baptist Church in Detroit, Michigan. She received her M.Div. from Morehouse School of Religion, ITC, Atlanta.

95

full impact of their last supper with Jesus. Once you know a little more about them, their behavior won't seem so out of place. Martha, the oldest of us three, acted like the typical oldest child—strong-willed and independent. I can remember her "giving orders" to Mary and me when we were kids. Martha had a very good business head, and would always go to the marketplace and conduct business for our household. Now that was rare for a woman to do in Palestine, but everyone in our small town knew Martha and came to respect her talents and gifts.

Mary was as different from Martha as night is from day. While Martha was outgoing and talkative, Mary was more of a loner—a deep thinker, you might say. You could almost always find her head in some book, reading or studying. That was also unheard of because Jewish custom frowns on women getting an education. Mary wasn't too interested in housework, and sometimes this was a source of frustration for Martha. Our home was a popular gathering spot whenever Jesus passed through Bethany, and Martha would wind up fussing because Mary would seldom help her get things ready.

It took Jesus to set Martha straight about Mary. And believe me, he was about the only one who could put Martha in her place. I was there when Jesus came to Mary's defense. It was one of those times Jesus and his disciples had come through town and stopped at our house to rest. Whenever Jesus stopped, people would gather and sit at his feet while he taught. A large number of people came by, and Martha was running around barking orders, while Mary sat at Jesus' feet. I'm quite sure Martha didn't expect Jesus to answer the way he did; and I must admit it was kind of funny to see Martha standing there with her mouth open, speechless. Even though she wasn't sitting at Jesus' feet, I'm sure Martha learned a lesson about priorities that day.

What seemed to make me the "talk of the town" was the fact that Jesus brought me back from the dead. It was Martha's persistence and faith, along with Mary's grief, that moved Jesus to perform that miracle. I'd caught a fever and got down low so quickly it surprised everybody. My sisters stood by my bed and whispered to each other that Jesus had to be called in. That's all I can remember, until I walked out of the grave. I'm told that Martha walked the dusty roads until she found Jesus outside Bethany. She talked openly with him, urging him to "do something." Never mind that women weren't supposed to talk to men in public—she was pleading for my life! And then there was Mary. Poor Mary, so tenderhearted and sensitive. Many of her friends came to comfort her because they knew she'd take my death hard. They were all there to see her tears of grief turn to tears of joy when I walked out of that tomb.

If we weren't before, Jesus and I became celebrities overnight. All those folks were witnesses to my death and resurrection. They went around telling anybody who would listen about Jesus' power. Now everybody wasn't thrilled that Jesus had done this miracle. The chief priests and the Pharisees didn't want the Romans to take away their status, so they got together and planned to kill Jesus and me, too.

I'll never forget that final night we had dinner with the Lord. All of us who believed in him came together to honor him, on a Saturday night. What was different about this last supper was that all of us who believed in him told stories about the miracles we'd seen, sang songs, and ate a meal. Everyone—men and women, old and young, rich and poor—were all in one place with one thing in common: love for Jesus.

The night of the dinner was a pretty happy one, but I got the feeling Jesus had a lot on his mind. As I think back about how he spoke to Judas, I'm almost positive he knew he was going to die soon. Right in the middle of the celebration, Mary poured a vial of *expensive* perfume on Jesus' feet. Then she wiped his feet with her hair. Most of us saw nothing wrong with what she did, probably because everyone knew just how much she loved Jesus. That's one thing I've learned about love—it will make you do strange things.

What happened at that supper was unusual. First, women were included. Second, Mary touched a man in public. Third, she took her hair down in public. All these actions were no-no's in Jewish culture. Judas was the only one who objected to Mary's use of her own gift. He later proved to be interested only in himself, and was the poorest disciple I can recall. What's ironic is that even though three years have passed since that last meal with Jesus, we disciples still get together on a regular basis, and each time we meet, we remember some of the things Jesus said to us then.

Jesus made it clear that he had no problem with Mary's act of devotion. Despite the fact that her behavior went against "tradition," his approval of her gift was all that mattered. Most folks at the supper probably didn't understand what Jesus meant about his burial

then; but we all pretty much understand now. What's more important is that by accepting Mary and Martha's gifts, Jesus showed us
that being male or female has nothing to do with discipleship. The
only things he asks of anyone who desires to be a servant of his is
love, obedience, and faithfulness.

My sisters showed all three gifts before Jesus left us; and they're
still hard at work as his followers. As for me, I'm trying my best to
live out my remaining days showing others the same love my two
sisters showed for me when they called on Jesus for help.

THE FOUR DAUGHTERS OF PHILIP, THE DEACON

SAMUEL D. PROCTOR

TEXT: Acts 21:8b, 9

One of the informal perquisites, added benefits, of being a preacher is the long tradition of being the welcomed guest in the homes of other preachers. With more use of hotels and motels, we are losing those precious moments of the richest fellowship we have known through spending a few hours or days with a treasured friend and his or her family. Paul's ministry was enriched by those long periods that he spent in the homes of his fellow servants on his three missionary journeys. He referred to the house of Stephanas in Corinth where they were *addicted* to the ministry to the saints; he spent much time in the home of Aquila and Priscilla; he stopped, also, in the home of one Justas; and we recall how Simon Peter lodged with Simon the tanner at his home in Joppa. Martin Luther King, Jr., used to tell us how his grandfather's home in Atlanta was a place where black leaders were made welcome, in the days of hotel segregation, and how he, as a boy, met and heard some of the renowned names of the day there.

It is no wonder that we find Paul in Caesarea, lodging for a few days at the home of Philip, who had been one of the first seven deacons of the church in Jerusalem. And the Bible tells us marvelous detail about Philip's family: he had four daughters—four—who had all become prophetesses.

When Paul found that out, he must have thought the same thing

---

Samuel D. Proctor is Pastor Emeritus of the Abyssinian Baptist Church in New York City; Visiting Professor of Preaching at Vanderbilt Divinity School; and Professor Emeritus, Rutgers University.

99

that flashes through our minds: this must have been a difficult situation for Philip and his wife. Here they were, advocates of a new and strange religion. Others may have ostracized them. And most likely, as a Christian, as a member of a small despised group, Philip did not have a well-paying job. It could not have been easy.

Caesarea, where Paul had stopped to rest and where Philip lived, was a seaport, a merchant-marine town, a place where people lived on short stays without their families, a wild town, a drinking town, a town of quick tricks, slick deals, and con games. This is where Philip lived with his four daughters, and they all became prophetesses, speaking for the Lord.

At best, rearing children is never easy. David, the sweet singer of Israel on whom God smiled with special favor, had one son, Absalom, who tried to kill him; and another, Solomon, who ended up with seven hundred wives and three hundred concubines—one thousand in all—out of his mind! Eli did well in helping Hannah get started with Samuel, but his own two sons, Hophni and Phinehas, were a disgrace to Eli and to his people. We read in Acts 19 of a man named Sceva, who had seven sons, and all seven were hustlers, con men, and vagabonds.

So, when we hear of these four prophetesses, the daughters of Philip, we are compelled to ponder what happened in Philip's house that did not happen in David's house, in Eli's house, or in the house of Mr. Sceva in Ephesus.

Likewise we ponder what must happen in our houses to change the frightening direction in which we are headed.

While the details are missing, the strong fact is that under the most difficult of circumstances Philip and his wife somehow came through with four daughters whose lives were committed to speak for the Lord. And even without the details, all of us who have had responsibility for guiding young lives as parents know that, for one thing, we have to recognize each child as a person, unique, different, authentic, valid, and consequential, a person demanding recognition, not a copy or a shadow of someone else.

All of us are created, framed, and detailed by the hand of God with our own personalities, our own DNA-genetic equipment, and with our own selective environment. We are bound to be different, and nothing like the love of sensitive parents can recognize and celebrate our unique personhood. They were four young women, and all four were prophetesses; but they had responded *uniquely* as they were loved one by one, and identified as persons of significance one by one.

When we read about and see so many wasted lives in our society, young women on drugs and becoming prostitutes only to pay for their drug habits, young men killing each other in senseless gang wars, persons being incarcerated for long terms for the most violent crimes against others, the conclusion that we are drawn to is that these lives never got beyond basic animal and instinct development. They were never ushered into true personhood, with the higher uses of the mind, with an appreciation of freedom and options, with a reflection on values and choices, with an awareness of what a life could become, with a vision of Jesus and his supreme and magnetic personality, calling us Godward, and toward our completion as sons and daughters of the living God. They never had their personhood recognized, cultivated, and celebrated. This must happen to us all one by one.

The name Philip is of Greek origin, from the verb *fileo,* meaning "I love." And the chances are that these daughters might have had Greek names. One could have been named Phyllis, *lover,* after her father; let us imagine that one would have been named Theodora, *one who honors God;* another Irene, *peaceful;* and another, Alethea, *truthful.* Phyllis could have started out playing rough games with boys, and rejecting "girlie" activities; Theodora could have been literary, memorizing the stories of the elders, and clinging to any scrap of papyrus with writing on it; Irene could have been housebound, close to her mother, enjoying domestic sorts of things like sewing and cooking; and Alethea could have been the first one to cling to the words and thoughts of Philip about Jesus Christ, and could have led the others closer to God and into their commitment to serve the Lord. And even though each had her own package of gifts, preferences, inhibitions, and abilities, they were so completely aware of the possibilities of a life given and endowed by God, that, although starting at different points, they chose to move toward the same purpose: to dedicate themselves to the service of God. They all spoke for the Lord!

Come next and see that while we are wishing for the best for our youth today, as we reflect on Philip's four daughters, we know also that Philip and his wife must have spent some time with these young women. Oh yes, Phyllis, Theodora, Alethea, and Irene were not in the streets at all hours of the day and night rearing themselves. In order to end up the way they did they had to be piloted gently out of the safe harbor of childhood, and guided carefully through the hidden rocks and treacherous shoals of adolescence, and then prepared for the high seas of adulthood with firm rudders and sturdy sails, and with a clear sense of direction. Parenting is serious in any age. And if we intend to do the best for our children, we try to transmit the best from our heritage and our culture to them, not the weakest and the worst.

I thank God that my parents were there for us, their children. Every night there were six pairs of elbows on the dining room table, Daddy was in one corner practicing his violin, and Mamma was in another sewing. We sang together, cried together, memorized Bible verses together, and looked at the future with wishful eyes together, beyond the awful Depression, the blatant racism, the hot, dusty streets, and the filth and violence that surrounded us in a small navy town.

And in order for Philip and his wife to give to the young church four daughters speaking for the Lord, they had to guarantee to each one that she was God's precious person, and patiently guide each one into the deep, safe channels of the finest human development. If we are to save our nation, the human race, the family of God, we will have to find out how Philip and his wife did it for their four daughters.

Finally, in order for these four young women to choose to answer the call to speak for the Lord, they must have seen how faithful their parents had been. Philip was one of the seven chosen to help Peter, James, John, and the others to get started after the cross and the resurrection. His daughters saw how he put down everything and gave himself to the work of spreading the Good News of God. These girls saw how their parents behaved with their lives threatened, with no money most of the time, with few friends, and thriving on the miraculous power of the Holy Spirit and the sustaining momentum that a life of prayer can provide. They saw it all. And they must have talked about it while waiting to fall asleep, and in early morning hours when the dew was gently dampening the ground, while birds played games darting about unmolested, and the sun was slowly lifting the last shadows of the night. Can't you hear those four girls, folded into each others legs, on a thin pallet covering a clay floor? How do Mommy and Daddy do it? They seem to be carried in the arms of God. Do they ever feel like giving up? Does loving Jesus Christ give you that much staying power? They act like Christ is alive in them! Suppose everyone loved God the way they do. How will the world know Jesus unless someone is willing to speak for the Lord? What would it be like if all four of us followed our parents?

Philip made the gospel real for them, and they found it to be a life-size challenge, a consuming calling, a worthwhile vocation for all four of them.

The best thing that any of us can do for our daughters is to share with them our faith, tell them about the rock on which we stand, the shelter that hides us from the storm, the bridge that brought us over deep waters, and the hills from which our help cometh.

Everyone needs a coherent view of the world, everyone needs a working belief system, everyone needs to know what to do with her solitude, everyone needs to know how to handle guilt and shame, defeat and failure, and how to call on the name of the Lord; and, everyone needs a Savior, a strong arm of deliverance. And everyone needs a story to tell, and a song to sing about how she got over. If you have nothing else to give to your daughters, give what Philip and his wife gave to their four daughters, the gospel, the Good News of the Son of God. And see how many will respond the same way Philip's daughters did: They all spoke for the Lord!

FAITHFUL RESISTANCE RISKING IT ALL: FROM EXPEDIENCE TO RADICAL OBEDIENCE

JACQUELYN GRANT

TEXT: Esther 4:13-16

More than anyone, Esther exemplifies what it means to move from concern for pure expedience to radical obedience.

The story is very familiar to all of us. Through the strategizing of Mordecai, her cousin and adoptive father, Esther found herself in the position of queen. The book begins with the dethronement of Queen Vashti for stepping out of her place—the prescribed place for women, and especially the king's wife. It goes on to reveal the king's search for a replacement—a new wife. Following Mordecai's instructions, Esther landed the coveted position of queen, wife of a king. When suddenly Haman's plan to destroy the Jews was made known, Mordecai proceeded to instruct Esther, by messenger, of her responsibility as a Jew.

The focus here is not on Mordecai's motives. Perhaps he was just protecting his own individual interests. Or perhaps it could be argued that he was simply an actor in God's providential plan to provide a savior of the Jews for such a time as that. I'd like to focus on Esther's obedience; we'll call it faithful resistance. Esther had two opportunities for obedience. The first was in Mordecai's initial plan to conceal her heritage and for her to "candidate" for the position of queen. It seems that Esther accepted this challenge with little or no resistance.

The second plan was more risky. Esther at this point was being called upon to stand up for the oppressed Jews. This identification as a Jew and the fact that she was a woman made it doubly risky. After

Jacquelyn Grant is Associate Professor of Systematic Theology at Interdenominational Theological Center in Atlanta, Georgia.

fasting and praying, Esther approached the king and saved her people from destruction. In spite of the positive result, it is clear that obedience in the second instance was a struggle: it required wrestling with what was at stake, primarily her life and personal security. Obedience here was not ordinary; it was faithful resistance and radical obedience.

This story affords us the opportunity to reflect upon the relationship between the personal and the political, the public and the private, the individual and the community. It enables us to focus upon the tensions between expedience and obedience, which can plague our decision-making process. In the Esther story, the tensions most concretely manifest themselves in the second decision of Esther's second opportunity for obedience. Esther had to reveal her identity, and that could cost her life.

Decision one (to conceal her identity in order to succeed) was a personal decision, with only personal glorification and advancement as the issue. Perhaps there was minimal tension here—that which may come from the concealment of one's identity—resulting primarily from the fear of being discovered. In the black experience in America, a comparable phenomenon has been known as "passing." For the most part this involved light-skinned black people who passed for the sake of personal gains, enjoying the benefits of white life in America.

Esther's second decision (to reveal her identity) was one that had a direct impact on the whole Jewish community. In the black community, many more could have passed than did, yet they saw their struggle as tied up with the struggle of black people. The movement of a minority of blacks to the status of middle-class should not cause us to forget that the masses of blacks are not there. They are still disproportionately poor, providing a pool of people from which comes a significant part of the increasingly permanent underclass.

It was not until Esther realized her *connectedness* that she was able to come to the point of declaring, "I shall obey the will of the higher authority. I shall approach the king on behalf of my people, and if I perish, I perish."

Only when Esther had succeeded in extricating herself from personal concerns was she free to affirm her real connectedness with her people and her real purpose in life. Mordecai had been right about her inability to escape, as well as about her being put in her position for just such a time and purpose as this.

The connectedness of life at various levels is demonstrated in this story. Here we see the interlinkages of racism and sexism. Esther could escape the harsh realities of anti-Semitism only for a season, as Mordecai said. And even though she was a queen, she was still a woman, and in jeopardy on occasion. She and her predecessor, Vashti, were under absolute male domination.

The connectedness of people is the only hope of the oppressed. Western culture's individualism must yield to the profound African understanding that says, "I am because we are." We are defined by our community, and if our community is negated, so are we. Thus Fannie Lou Hamer could say to the first African-American congressman from Mississippi since Reconstruction, "We marched on the white folks to make them do right. . . . If you don't do right, we're going to march on you, too." She was saying to him that he is because we are, because the community struggled and fought for rights denied us as a people for centuries.

African-American womanist scholars have begun to emphasize this type of interconnectedness. Perceiving the interstructuring of racism, classism, and sexism, they have insisted that the "we-ness" informs the "I-ness," even though the "I-ness" is our concrete starting place for all theological analysis. Our one concrete starting place locates us in the whole of reality. From there we recognize that the struggle for liberation is a global struggle. The oppression of blacks in the United States is not unrelated to the oppression of blacks in South Africa and the oppression of the indigenous peoples of Latin America or Australia.

We are as connected together as the links in a chain, which is broken when only one link is broken. Our resistance must be done in unity, but Esther reminds us that it must also be done in faith. She could not know the outcome of her risk taking, but she knew that she must act. As we say, she did not know what the future held, but she did know who held the future. On this basis her obedient resistance could escalate to a radical level. It is summed up in the defiant and faithful declaration, "If I perish, I perish."

Risking it all in faithful resistance to the oppressive and debilitating structures may mean losing a privileged position. For Esther it could have meant the loss of her place as queen in the royal court, or even being booted out altogether. She could have been sentenced to death. But, as Martin Luther King, Jr., used to say, "If you haven't found anything worth dying for, life isn't worth living."

When Esther understood her connectedness, she understood what had to be done. When we understand how our destiny is tied up with that of black people in South Africa, then we will know what we must do. When we understand that our destiny is tied up with that of a homeless mother and children in southwest Atlanta, we'll know what we must do. When we sense our links with Native Americans on reservations, and poor people in Appalachia, and migrant workers across the southern United States, we'll know what we must do.

This risking it all will also mean that men ministers will stand with women in ministry even when they are threatened with expulsion from the ministerial alliance, and with ostracism from the "brethren."

Risking it all will mean that women will have the audacity to preach when some who presume to know the mind of God declare that they can't. These faithful women will step out of the roles prescribed by a patriarchal society, under which the masses of women are suffering. Their faithful resistance does not mean that they will not lose anything. Indeed, Esther could have lost her all, but in fact she won.

When you resist faithfully, when you risk it all, I can't guarantee that you won't lose anything. All I can say is that I serve one who gave up his very life and went to the cross for all humanity. And I stand in a tradition of black women who have declared that if Jesus goes with them, they'll go anywhere.

Their record inspires. Harriet Tubman said she would go, and she conducted hundreds to freedom by the Underground Railroad. Sojourner Truth spoke out fearlessly against racism and sexism. Jarena Lee preached with power even when the church said she could not. Marie Stewart taught and made public addresses when "colored" or "Negro" women were not supposed to. Mary McLeod Bethune founded a school on one dollar and fifty cents and faith. Fannie Lou Hamer challenged a nation sick with sin, from her place among poor women in the state of Mississippi. All these and many, many more took the risks.

But my faith tells me that if we, like Esther, remain faithful to the struggle, we may lose many things, but there is promise of gain.

We'll lose despair, but we have the promise of hope.
We'll lose hatred, but there is the promise of love.
We'll lose ignorance, but we'll gain human insight.
We'll lose separation, but we have the promise of unity.
We'll lose fear, but we'll have the promise of courage.
We may even lose earthly life, but we have the promise of life
    eternal.

Faithful resistance does not take away the risks, but it keeps us
headed for the promise.

We've come this far by faith
Leaning on the Lord,
Trusting in the Lord's holy Word;
The Lord's never failed us yet.

WOMEN MINISTERS: HEIRS OF THE PROMISE— ON FIRE, UNDER FIRE

DELORES H. CAUSION CARPENTER

TEXT: Hebrews 10:35

Women Ministers: Heirs of the Promise—On Fire, Under Fire addresses the historical reality of African-American women in ministry. Women ministers have played a significant role in my life. I stand upon the broad shoulders of those who have gone on to glory. Four women continue to give me sustenance, courage, and strength to believe in my own calling and the legitimate place of women in the ordained and pastoral ministry.

Reverend Sister Mary Johnson was the pastor's daughter and one of the assistant ministers of St. Paul Freewill Baptist Church. She preached every fifth Sunday, which was always Youth Day. She was also the adult advisor to the Young People's Christian League and its annual convention. As a teenager, I was fascinated with Reverend Sister Johnson. She was a strikingly beautiful and well-dressed woman. She had lived in New York City, and there she had met many Pentecostal women ministers. As a girl she had been diagnosed as having leukemia. Her family had been told that she would only live to be eighteen years old. But through her faith she lived into her forties. She was frequently hospitalized, so it was a joy to see her coming into the sanctuary, a tambourine in her hand. It always meant a difference in the worship service. Her testimony of God's healing hand in her life and her love for young people added a special dimension to the congregation.

Delores H. Causion Carpenter is Pastor of the Michigan Park Christian Church, Disciples of Christ, and is Associate Professor of Religious Education at Howard University School of Divinity.

111

I knew I could learn much about God through her. It was my last visit with her in the hospital that was to change my life. As she lay dying, she looked at me and said, "Delores, why don't you do what God is calling you to do?" Several times before she had asked me, "Delores, do you have something to tell me?" These were questions that I could not escape. They left me speechless. However, they were to be a gateway out of the dark night of the soul. At Reverend Sister Johnson's funeral, I was to speak on behalf of the youth. When I rose to speak, I could not say what I had prepared. But rather I confessed, "God has called me to preach. Reverend Sister Johnson encouraged me to do what God has been calling me to do!" I felt as if a great load had been lifted from my shoulders. At the same time, it was as if I had reached down and picked up a mantle that she had left behind.

Reverend Sister Johnson dreamed of a day when things would be different for women in ministry. She might have expressed her sentiments this way:

> Come on; you can make it. Come on through hard times. Keep the fire in your souls; the prize is at the end.

My grandmother, Mrs. Sarah Causion, was a woman who had a third-grade education. She had lost a leg when she was eight years old. Later she was widowed and had six children to raise. In spite of these limitations, she found time to write religious tracts. They consisted of listings of biblical texts according to certain topics. They almost always dealt with salvation and being born again. She loved the Lord and she taught us children to use our gifts, no matter how small, to the glory of God. She organized her grandchildren to sing gospel songs. On Sunday mornings, we went to the tuberculosis ward at City Hospital in Baltimore, before most people were even getting out of bed. She took us to nursing homes. We accompanied her in her exhortations. She was noted as a fervent pray-er. She was known for her prophecies and her healing hands. My grandmother consulted with spiritualists, took Communion from the Baptist deacons, studied with the Jehovah's Witnesses, and put up a tent on the vacant Masonic lot next door so that Pentecostal preachers could conduct revival services.

Not only that, she took care of other folks' children, when their parents were unable to care for them. She always had an extra place set at the table for guests who dropped by.

It was after I was ordained as a Baptist minister that "G-mama" sought some kind of ministerial status. Looking through her tracts, one sees the progression from Mother Causion, to Missionary Causion, to Evangelist Causion and finally to Reverend Sister Causion. It was through my grandmother that I met my first collective of women ministers, the Baltimore Women Ministers' Alliance. They had the authority to ordain women ministers and to register them with the city government. This is how my grandmother received the title "Reverend." Her own Missionary Baptist Church could only grant her missionary status.

And what do I remember of this network of women ministers? I remember how they nurtured and supported one another. I remember how they held forth in special services, often on Sunday afternoons or during midweek. Frequently, the only people in attendance at these services were grandmothers and grandchildren. Sometimes other family members and neighbors would come. They came together from all different kinds of churches. Half the time, the churches that the women ministered in were storefront and house churches. They traveled the East Coast. Occasionally, one of the group would be asked to appear on a program or preach at one of the larger churches. Usually these were Women's Day programs, revival services, or other special occasions.

The ministers would consult with each other about the contents of their sermons. Some were flamboyant, some were accused of trying to act like men, and some appeared eccentric. But they were ecumenical and they were committed to one primary task: to reach some lost soul, to lead the person to Christ.

Before my grandmother died, she promised me that things would be better for women ministers in the future. She valued education and she taught me that an education would be the key to unlocking many doors. She said, "Don't be moved. Be like a tree planted by the water." Today in heaven she is saying . . .

> Come on; you can make it. Come on through hard times. Keep the fire
> in your souls; the prize is at the end.

I met Reverend Sister Dorothy Stewart at St. Paul Freewill Baptist Church. I was youth advisor to her two children. She always came to the Wednesday evening Bible study and prayer meetings. She followed me in and out of many churches from revival to revival,

from Bible study to Bible study, from Women's Day to Youth Day.
After I married and moved to St. Louis, Sister Stewart was licensed
and ordained to Christian ministry. She worked hard in her church,
and she was serving as the assistant minister when the pastor died.
She had given leadership throughout his illness and during the
months of his absence. But when the time came for the funeral, the
ministers' conference sent in ministers, male ministers, who totally
disregarded her. She was not even invited to sit near the pulpit with
the other ministers. She went unrecognized.

Sister Stewart and I would often observe the discrimination shown
to women in the ministry. There was one time of the year when this
was especially pronounced in a large downtown church we used to
like to visit together. New Year's Eve was the only opportunity for
the female missionaries to speak. They'd line up on the pulpit and
each of them would have a limited amount of time. They would
preach hard, and few could ever finish. Sister Stewart and I would
discuss whether this phenomenon was ever going to change. But
Sister Stewart knew that it would. She'd tell me, "Dee, if you were
here, they would have asked you to sit in the pulpit. They would
have recognized you. Things will be different for you." Sister Stewart
died strong in the faith, a good friend to the end. And she too is in
heaven saying . . .

> Come on; you can make it. Come on through hard times. Keep the fire
> in your souls; the prize is at the end.

Finally, I lift up Joyce. Joyce was a second-career woman, having
spent many years as legal secretary to a judge in Indiana. She was a
distinguished lay woman of the 1970s in our denomination. I met her
while serving with her on the general board; we were in the same
section. She was articulate; she was a good thinker. She was the
secretary of section one. Later, she was elected moderator for her
region of Indiana, one of the largest. When Joyce decided to accept
her call to ministry, she enrolled in seminary. But during her studies
she had recurring episodes of cancer, which would render her sometimes up and sometimes down. She had to learn to take the good days
and be down on the bad days. But her beautiful spirit was an inspira-
tion to all who knew her. It was a miracle that she finished seminary.
It was a miracle that she was ordained. She had just begun receiving
requests to preach in other parts of the country when she grew ill.

The last time I visited with Joyce, she told me her work was not yet done, and she was looking forward to speaking in California. Joyce never made it to California. She died without being able to finish the work she so desired.

Their work is done. Ours has just begun. We are called by God. We are anointed with the Holy Spirit. But we are also inspired by the spirit of women ministers who have gone before us. For these four all died hoping and believing a promise—a promise of a more inclusive church. They did not live to see the changes of the late eighties, the 1990s and the twenty-first century, when women will be 51 percent of the labor force in America.

This quartet in heaven plants commitment, confidence, and courage in my heart. It makes it perfectly clear to me that we cannot acquiesce to past inequities and injustices, for we have this promise given to us by them, and given to them by God. Embodied in these sisters of the Spirit is the hope that African-American women ministers will receive the blessings of opportunity, the blessings of fulfillment, and the blessings of service in both private and public arenas. We know that their dreams and hopes in ministry gushed forth from God, as part of God's creating, renewing, reconciling, and liberating work of the twentieth and twenty-first centuries.

Hebrews 10:35-36 speaks to us: "Cast not away therefore your confidence, which hath great recompence of reward. For ye have need of patience, that, after ye have done the will of God, ye might receive the promise" (KJV). Truly we are heirs of a promise. And we have a God whose promises we can rely on. As Miriam Winter affirms: "[We] believe in a God / . . . who suffers whenever / humanity suffers, / . . . whenever [anyone] / is violated, / mutilated, / or handled with disrespect, / who stands beside us and within us / whenever we lose our nerve. / [We] believe in a God / . . . who mediates hope / that rises above the limits / of time / and place, / who is durable / and vulnerable, / who sometimes shows a masculine mood, / more often / a feminine face. / [We] believe in a God / who holds us all / in Her everlasting arms, / who gathers us protectively / to the shelter of Her wings, / who binds our wounds, / dries our tears, / and promises better things."[1]

---

[1]Miriam Therese Winter, *Womanprayer, Womansong.* Copyright © Medical Mission Sisters, 1987.

In my denomination, the Christian Church (Disciples of Christ), 14 percent of all licensed and ordained ministers are women; 207 serve as pastors and 138 are associate pastors. In 1989, 30–50 percent of all seminarians were women. This challenges the assumption that women in the ministry are just a passing fad. Too frequently, congregations lament a lack of qualified leadership in the church and then ignore, at their own peril, the effective leadership qualifications of clergy women. One in every four seminary graduates today is a woman. In 1989, at Howard University School of Divinity, the three ranking students were women. Some of the best and brightest candidates for positions of professional, ordained leadership are female. But clergy women are facing problems today. Some of them can't find church-related work. Their salaries are lower than that of their male counterparts. Often women are forced to work in congregations that do not offer the kind of challenge that matches their skills. There is still much work to be done, but the number of women who are expressing a determination to serve God, to serve the world in the name of Jesus Christ, and to serve the Body of Christ is steadily increasing.

In Luke 12:54-56, Jesus said to the multitude, "When you see a cloud rising in the west, you say at once, 'A shower is coming'; and so it happens. And when you see the south wind blowing, you say, 'There will be scorching heat'; and it happens. You hypocrites! You know how to interpret the appearance of earth and sky; but why do you not know how to interpret the present time?" With women in ministry in mind, why do some not know how to interpret the present time?

If I were asked to give a hermeneutic of the present time, regarding women in ministry, it would be this: "Women on fire, under fire."

This powerful and pervasive trend among hundreds of gifted women is similar to Jeremiah, who holds the word within his heart, as it were, a devouring fire that he cannot constrain. "If I say, 'I will not mention him, or speak any more in his name," there is in my heart as it were a burning fire shut up in my bones, and I am weary with holding it in, and I cannot" (Jeremiah 20:9). As I speak with women ministers who are on fire with the Spirit of God, that Spirit is captured in the word "pregnant," anxious to come forth, and it is not their own word, but God's word.

Jeremiah tried to resist this calling. He said he was too young, but

God told him, "Before I formed you in your mother's womb, I knew you. I consecrated you to myself. I've been knowing you longer than you've known yourself. And what I'm trying to get you to do, Jeremiah, is to see you as I see you" (Jeremiah 1:5-10, paraphrased). And I believe that is what God is trying to get women in ministry to do today. God is calling women, filling them with a living Word and trying to get them to see their possibility in God. God is trying to have my sisters see themselves, not as men see them, but as God sees them.

Marie Stewart can help us out. She was on fire in the 1800s. She said, "I believe that for wise and holy purposes best known to himself, he hath unloosed my tongue and put his word in my mouth in order to confound and put all those to shame who have risen up against me. For he has clothed my face with steel and lined my forehead with brass. He has put his testimony within me. Engraved his seal on my forehead."[2]

Women are on fire, under fire. This is the hermeneutic of today. Jesus calls us to watch the signs of the time. Watch these women on fire, under fire. Some don't believe they should be ordained. Some don't believe they should pastor. But still God anoints them. Still their cups overflow.

Again in the words of Miriam Winter: "Two women care, four women dare, / and ten will follow after. / Two are few, but four are more, / and ten times ten worth waiting for. / A million strong on a single song, / soon the whole world sings along, / and a new day dawns. / Out there on your own, / know that you are not alone. / Look around and see / signs of solidarity. / When you feel harassed, / first in line, yet always last, / don't withdraw and hide. / Find a friend to stand beside. / Two women care, four women dare, / and ten will follow after. / Two are few, but four are more, / and ten times ten worth waiting for. / A million strong on a single song, / soon the whole world sings along, / and a new day dawns."[3]

---

[2]From 1831 pamphlet "Religion and the Pure Principles of Morality."

[3]Miriam Therese Winter, *Womanprayer, Womansong.* Copyright © Medical Mission Sisters, 1987.

MINISTRY ON THE EVE OF
A NEW MILLENNIUM

JAMES A. FORBES, JR.

TEXT: Revelation 20

Brothers and sisters, I want to speak to you on the theme, Ministry on the Eve of a New Millennium. At the end of this decade, a most significant event will take place. On the last day of December 1999, we'll move toward the remaining moments of the year. In the final seconds, digital clocks will advance from 1999 to 2000—the beginning of a new millennium. Can you imagine what that New Year celebration will be like? Think of the weeks, months, and even years of preparation as that moment approaches. Times Square will not be large enough to hold the people. Neither Times Square nor New York City will hold a monopoly as the place to be when the millennium comes. Well before the stroke of twelve, arrangements will have been made for welcoming the new age around the world. Expeditions will have arrived at the closest point to the international date line to enable folks to say, "I was there first." Is it not also likely that there will be capsules orbiting in outer space, the better to greet the brand-new day?

Actually, I can't think of any person of reasonable health and awareness who will be able to be indifferent to that once-in-ten-lifetimes opportunity. I believe that the coming of the millennium will be the major event for many, many years—from now until that time. I believe it has already manifested its extraordinary power to spark imagination and hope.

James A. Forbes, Jr., is the Senior Pastor of the Riverside Church in New York City, and Former Engle Professor of Preaching, Union Theological Seminary, New York City.

Five years ago, *Essence Magazine* for today's black woman included an article on black America in the year 2000, "What the Trends Say." The trends say that you've got to acknowledge that we must seize the opportunity now, for perhaps the most critical task we face is to try to make it to 2000 because, at that time, 53 percent of the country's largest cities will be dominated by blacks, 38 of these in the South. There will be 28.6 million Hispanics. But 12 out of every 100,000 black men will kill themselves. As we progress in business and social circles, we isolate ourselves from our supportive family and friends. We've got a lot of work to do, said the magazine, if we are going to make it to the year 2000.

And my sense is that, whatever the secular press has had to say, the year 2000 will touch us in ways that persons unfamiliar with the Bible will not understand. In the book of Revelation, we have been led to watch thousand-year increments. We have a kind of eschatological weight riding on this thousand-year time span. I think we need to be aware that according to the Bible, we are supposed to watch out for the thousand-year time because something very significant will happen. In the twentieth chapter of Revelation we read that the beginning of the millennium is special, even though we can't be sure what that year is going to bring.

This is conflictory. We do not know whether the year 2000 is the time when the "dragon" is going to be bound or loosed. One of our seminary students, before a committee examining him for ordination, was asked what his position was with respect to millennialism. He didn't even know what it was. He said. "What do you mean?" "Well, what is your stand in regard to the millennium? Are you a premillennialist, a postmillennialist or an amillennialist?" He thought for a moment and said, "I'm a panmillennialist." They asked him, "What is that?" He said, "I think everything's going to pan out all right."

Let me make it very clear that it is not my mission today to reintroduce apocalyptic language, nor to debate the merits of a particular school of eschatological thought. Rather, I want to share a strong impression that the year 2000 is a powerful moment in history that has already started to beckon to us, and will increasingly place before us an invitation we will find difficult to ignore. It will become a siren call, luring us into its perils or promises. The prospects of attending Celebration 2000 will occasion fresh visioning, will spark utopian impulses, will provoke cosmic critique, will stimulate goal setting and the quest for new ways and means. Ultimate questions will be raised about the meaning of human history everywhere. Theologians and people in the street, the pulpits, and the pews, will begin to ask where God fits in, what matters and why, who belongs and how to survive, who is for us and who is against us. We will experience conspiracies, tyrannies, breakthroughs, and breakdowns. So, I have come to extend to each of you, the brothers and the sisters, an invitation to Celebration 2000.

Be assured the event is going to happen. I simply want to invite you, and encourage you, to come to that event. Let me tell you, it's a powerful moment just to contemplate it, and let me suggest why so much energy is going to be spent around 2000. The year 2000 touches two vectors at the core of our being. Observe that moving from 1999 to 2000 is both advancement and return. Moving from the one to the two is advancement. But from 999 to 000 is return. So here is a moment that allows us to back up and advance at the same time. It is micro and at the same time macro. Life at a speck and at a span at the same time. It has short-run and long-run thinking. We get a chance to look at things from the perspective of the angels. You understand in one-thousand-year increments. We sing about it, but have you *thought* about it? "A thousand ages in thy sight are like an evening gone short as the watch that ends the night before the rising sun."[1] Do you want to be there at Celebration 2000? I definitely plan to be there, Lord willing.

There is a minor detail that I want to go back to. The Revelation said we do not know whether it will be a time of celebration or a time of lamentation, but John, the revelator, gives an impression that, quite possibly, we could make a difference. This is why he records Jesus' words: "Be faithful unto death, and I will give you the crown of life" (Revelation 2:10). Although we're not totally in charge, if we could get a critical mass the size of the martyrs, the saints, and the servants of the church through the ages, and if this mass leans toward the conditions that would lead us toward celebration, we just might experience celebration rather than lamentation and woe.

This is the reason I really want to talk to you. I want to find out just what kind of year we can expect it to be. It is my conviction that

---

[1]From the hymn, "O God Our Help in Ages Past," by Isaac Watts.

between now and the year 2000, analysis of where we are and what we've got to do will have to be discussed wherever we gather; the issues before us are so urgent, we ought to secure insights wherever we can.

With any invitation, you usually will have an RSVP. So far as I am concerned, the *R* may call to mind a number of issues. Some folks say reconciliation. Other people say it's got to do with racial issues. But the answer that came up for me, in terms of whether we're going to get there, has to do with resources. We can plan all we want to, but if we don't deal with resources, we're in trouble. What are the resources that God has placed on the earth? What are the effective means of availing ourselves of these resources without exhausting them? What about resource distribution? What about the lifestyle and the consumption in our time? Finding solutions to these problems will require diligent effort on everyone's part; we cannot afford to ignore the valuable contribution that women preachers can make to these issues. Unless we figure out a way to find out what God had in mind as to who should be restored, unless we find a better way to receive the resources without depleting the resources that God has given, unless we find a way to get around to better use of resources, we might run out of some crucial resources needed for the celebration.

Now for the letter *S.* There are many different things that we could say, but let me propose this concern. We live in an increasingly secular society. And the faith basis of our common life has been eroded through the years. Therefore, we are going to definitely need *spiritual revitalization.* I'm not going to say much about what that means just now, but until the spirit of truth, justice, equality, love, and peace spreads across the land, I don't know whether we're going to make it. We must not limit ourselves in our search for this revitalization by overlooking what our preaching sisters have to say on the subject. Unless there is a mighty spiritual revitalization in our time, the future is bleak.

I have no question about what the letter *V* points me to. I go for *value.* This is a time when we, with our technological resources, our new freedom frontiers of the future, must have our values clear. What used to be will not be adequate for the new millennium. We will discover that what we had back there only gives us a head start beginning for right now. What does it mean to be human? Who ought to be included into human communities? What kind of protections of rights will be necessary? What kind of use of our own liberties can be promoted if we have Christian values? We've got to look at values. And we've got to hear the message of women preachers so that our set of values is not partial, but complete. How about the values for what the configuration is of the families within which people are going to be living? What about values as to what we say no to and what we say yes to? We've got all sorts of values we must deal with.

Everybody's probably talking about *P.* We must deal with *peace,* but *peace* is more *problematical* in this *pluralistic* age. We have a whole lot of folks who want peace, but they have different frames of reference, different values, different outlooks, different approaches. So my belief is we're going to have to get a little more *pluralistic sophistication.* We must learn how to live in a community with different kinds of people, if we are going to make it to the year 2000.

Brothers and sisters, I have not exhausted the list. The exact composition of the list is not the real issue. In order to get to the year 2000, we need a committee. I want to recruit each of you to be on the committee for the celebration. Are you and your people ready for the great celebration? Are you ready to use *all* of the human resources God has provided in order to accomplish this massive preparation?

Can you look at the vast, virtually untapped reservoir of talented and dedicated women, and decline to let them share in such crucial responsibilities as the preaching? Dare you risk the dangers of a less-than-adequate reading of *all* of the Bible, as you make your decision to exclude anyone? Or will you receive and cherish *all* whom God has called to take part on this huge committee for this unthinkably great task? More than just to acquiesce, our job is to help them get ready.

If you accept a part of this committee work, it will require that *you* too be involved in sharing the Good News. Don't waste a sermon. Tell the world what the vision is, what God's provisions are for whomever God calls—male or female—what the economic justice must be, and what the principles of life must be. Every time you preach, you're trying to get folks ready for Celebration 2000. Our people will have to learn how to respect and trust each other, learn how to take different approaches to achieve the same objectives. We have to be aware of resource development, redistribution methodology, and how to expand the guest list. God will call off the event, if the right folks have not been invited.

Don't worry. It's a lot of hard work. I don't know how we're going to do it. I think the best way to get you ready to be on the committee is to tell you who the Chairperson is. The Chairperson is the Director of Cosmic Celebration. This Person was there in Creation, was there when God created a nation at the Red Sea, and was there at Calvary for the drama of salvation. Right now, the Chairperson is waiting for a major event called Cosmic Consummation; therefore, our little year 2000 will be an easy matter for that Chairperson to handle.

Brothers and sisters, why don't you commit yourselves to the Holy Spirit who's got the plan in hand, looking for a woman and a man who will help take care of business? I would like to repeat the good news that you're invited to the year 2000. Let me make this clear: I don't know what my life is going to be, but I plan to be there. If you come to Times Square and you don't see me, don't stop. Come on out to the international date line. I may be there. But if you don't find me any of those places, come on up to a "city four-square"; I'll be waiting up there.

THE UNEXPECTED POSSIBILITIES OF GOD

SUSAN NEWMAN HOPKINS

TEXT: Luke 1:26-38; 46-55

Events thought impossible transpire every day. In the year 1989 alone the world witnessed the opening of the Berlin Wall that divided East and West Germany for twenty-eight years. Russia and the United States began to appear more like allies than nemeses. In South Africa, for the first time since the National Party of apartheid came to power in 1948, there surfaced a widespread acceptance of the need to change. Under the reform-minded government of State President F.W. de Klerk, Nelson Mandela, the black revolutionary imprisoned for sedition twenty-seven years ago, became a free man. And maybe most unusual of all, for the first official time since Harriet Tubman, a woman, Linda Bray, led thirteen thousand U.S. soldiers in an invasion in Panama on December 20, 1989.

We become accustomed to the routines of life and often forget to expect change. When change occurs, we view it as surprising, shocking, and impossible. Yet as Christians we believe in a God who is able to do exceeding abundantly, above all that we ask or think, even in changing our rigid traditions about limitations on women.

In the first chapter of the Gospel of Luke, we see something totally unexpected. In Nazareth a young virgin girl, Mary, is engaged to Joseph. Everything in her life is going well until the angel Gabriel unexpectedly greets her, saying, "Hail, thou that art highly favoured, the Lord is with thee: blessed art thou among women" (v. 28, KJV). Mary is deeply troubled by the angel's greeting. Yet Gabriel says,

---

Susan Newman Hopkins is Chaplain at Hood College in Frederick, Maryland. She received her D.Min. from United Theological Seminary in Dayton, Ohio.

"Do not be afraid, Mary, for you have found favor with God. And behold, you will conceive in your womb and bear a son, and you shall call his name Jesus." Gabriel continues, "He will be great, and will be called the Son of the Most High; and the Lord God will give to him the throne of his father David, and he will reign over the house of Jacob forever; and of his kingdom there will be no end" (vv. 30-33).

Mary is shocked, maybe insulted, even though this is an angel from heaven. "How can this be? I've never been with any man. How can I conceive a son?" So Gabriel explains, "The Holy Spirit will come upon you, and the power of the Most High will overshadow you; therefore the child to be born will be called holy, the Son of God. . . . For with God nothing will be impossible" (vv. 35-37).

Here she is, a very young woman, living her life as other women her age, living the "expected" daily life of women in her culture and time. And without any warning, without any provocation or petitions to God on her part, Mary is chosen by God to bear the Son of God, the Living Word.

Gabriel tells her that she is the favored one of God. She is whom God has chosen to fulfill God's will. "Why can't this wait until *after* I am married to Joseph?" She is full of fear and apprehension. Mary knows what people will say. She knows the laws of her culture, race, and religion. Worst of all, she knows that being found pregnant before marriage means a sentence of death according to the Law.

The Jewish matrimonial procedure of betrothal consists of two steps: a formal exchange of consent before witnesses (Malachi 2:14) and the subsequent taking of the bride to the groom's family home (Matthew 25:1-13). The first step is as legally binding as the second. The betrothal is usually entered into when the girl is between twelve and thirteen years old, and gives the young man rights over the girl. She is his wife, and any violation of his marital rights could be punished as adultery. Yet the wife continues to live at her own family home for about a year. Then the formal taking of the bride to the husband's family home occurs when he assumes her support. According to the Hebrew Law, if a bride is not a virgin, "They shall bring out the young woman to the door of her father's house, and the men of her city shall stone her to death," (Deuteronomy 22:20, 21). Mary fears for her life. The scandal would be downright torture, but she could survive scandal. However, the threat of death and the shame to her family is unthinkable!

Legion are the women throughout human history who have been given a vision of the utterly unexpected to fulfill. Oftentimes there were only a few who shared the vision or believed in the dream. Could it be possible that God does call women to preach? Could it be possible that God endows them richly and fruitfully employs their gifts for ministry? Mary, after hearing the news that she was chosen to bear the child of God without the involvement of a man, asks, "How shall this be?" Gabriel answers, "The Holy Spirit will come upon you, and the power of the Most High will overshadow you; therefore the child to be born will be called holy, the Son of God."

Women who feel called by God to preach ask the same question. "How shall this be? How is it that I am to stand and speak on behalf of God?" Often, the question is born not out of an uncertainty of gender roles, but from the realization that God is holy and we are sinful human beings with faults like everyone else. What makes us worthy? Like the prophet Isaiah, standing in the temple before the presence of God, we too say, "Woe is me! For I am undone, because I am a woman of unclean lips, and I dwell in the midst of a people of unclean lips." "How shall this be?" we ask. It is so because of the Holy Spirit's anointing. "The Holy Spirit will come upon you and the power of the Most High will overshadow you."

We try to control just about everything in our lives, but we cannot control the Spirit of God. We cannot tell God what to do, whom to use, and when or where to do God's will. The gospel of Jesus Christ is preached with such power that men and women, boys and girls come down the aisles of our churches every Sunday, accepting Jesus Christ as their Savior. God's Spirit is powerful enough to seek and to save, powerful enough to wash us of all sins, in the waters of baptism, but many still believe that God's Spirit is not powerful enough to use those redeemed souls to proclaim the Good News that resides within their hearts.

When the possibilities of God are about to descend upon us, things that we do not understand happen. On the day of Pentecost, when the Holy Spirit fell upon everyone in the upper room, they began to proclaim God's praises in many tongues. The people said, "They must be drunk." But Peter stood and said, "Men of Judea and all who dwell in Jerusalem . . . these men are not drunk, as you suppose

. . . this is what was spoken by the prophet Joel: 'And in the last days it shall be, God declares, that I will pour out my Spirit upon all flesh, and your sons and your daughters shall prophesy, and your young men shall see visions, and your old men shall dream dreams; yea, and on my menservants and my maidservants in those days I will pour out my Spirit; and they shall prophesy' " (Acts 2:14-18).

When the power of the Most High overshadows you, that which is created inside is holy. Mary, overshadowed by the Spirit of God, conceives Jesus, the Christ. Women, anointed by the Spirit of God, conceive within their spirits the Good News that must be proclaimed. As the prophet Jeremiah said, "[God's Word was] in my heart as it were a burning fire shut up in my bones, and I am weary with holding it in, and I cannot" (Jeremiah 20:9).

If Mary only thinks about herself and her reputation, she may refuse to be the vessel for such an event. It is no secret that in the first century many people were resourceful about ridding their betrothed daughters of unwanted pregnancies. Yet Mary believes in God. She believes that this child within her womb would save her people. She trusts in God to take care of her, and it never crosses her mind to do away with the work of God.

But that doesn't make it less astounding. It is amazing! God, the Creator of the heavens and earth, chooses to come to suffering humanity through the body of a woman! The One who created light out of darkness, the One who said "Let there be," and worlds leapt into existence, the One who created man and woman in the beginning, from the dust of the earth—that One now chooses to come to us through a female vessel, a woman hardly thought to be fully human in her time, a person with no rights, oft abused, and even saleable as property. The *Living Word* is to be delivered by a lowly maiden of the countryside!

One cannot help but empathize with the baffling emotions Mary would be feeling at a time like this. And any woman called by God to an unexpected place in God's plan feels the same fear of people, struggling against the sheer awe at the call of God. She dares not say no to the very emissary of God, so she reverently and, yes, timidly responds, "Behold the handmaid of the Lord; be it unto me according to thy word" (v. 38, KJV).

She answers yes, but she still needs help to embrace fully the unexpected possibilities, so she is led to go to the hill country to see

Cousin Elizabeth. This much older woman's baby unexpectedly stirs in the womb at the first sound of Mary's greeting, and this saintly senior sister is filled with the Holy Ghost. It turns out that Elizabeth already knows about the angel, and she gives her young cousin a loud and warm and wonderful blessing. There is a fiery certainty about it, and Mary's fears and forebodings melt away. Everything is all right now; the very Spirit of God has sealed the call of God.

I know the feeling of being confirmed in the call, even when the messenger is unaware. Last summer I worshiped at a church where the preacher is known to be struggling with his feelings about women in the ministry. But little did he know as he announced his text, that more than any other sermon I'd heard, his sermon sealed my convictions to preach undauntedly as long as I have breath. His text was Mark 8:36, 38, "For what shall it profit . . . if [you] shall gain the whole world, and lose [your] soul? Whosoever therefore shall be ashamed of me and of my words in this adulterous and sinful generation; of him [or her] also shall the Son of man be ashamed, when he cometh in the glory of his Father with the holy angels" (KJV).

Mary, filled with joy over being chosen by God, stood up to prophesy and, remembering Hannah's song of praise, took her text from I Samuel 2:1-10 and began singing a new variation on an ancient theme. "My soul doth magnify the Lord. And my spirit hath rejoiced in God my Saviour. For he hath regarded the low estate of his handmaiden: for, behold, from henceforth all generations shall call me blessed. For he that is mighty hath done to me great things; and holy is his name. And his mercy is on them that fear him from generation to generation. He hath shewed strength with his arm; he hath scattered the proud in the imagination of their hearts. He hath put down the mighty from their seats, and exalted them of low degree. He hath filled the hungry with good things; and the rich he hath sent empty away. He hath [helped] his servant Israel, in remembrance of his mercy; As he spake to our fathers, to Abraham, and to his seed forever" (KJV).

If I may take a flight of imagination, I see Mary "opening the doors of the church," inviting all women and men to come and follow a God of unexpected possibilities. I can see them coming down through the ages. Women and men who have accomplished things in spite of what others have called "the impossible." I see them coming from slavery—Sojourner Truth, Gabriel Prosser. I see them coming from the arts—Marian Anderson, James Baldwin, Todd Duncan, Maya Angelou. I see them coming from the halls of education—Mary McLeod Bethune, George Washington Carver, Nannie Helen Burroughs. I see them coming from the scales of justice—Patricia Roberts Harris, Barbara Jordan, David Dinkens, and Douglas Wilder. I see them coming from the publications—Frederick Douglass, Ida B. Wells Barnett, and John H. Johnson. I see them coming from the athletic arena—Joe Louis, Althea Gibson, Jesse Owens and Florence Griffith Joyner. And yes, I see them coming from the church—Jarena Lee, Richard Allen, Martin Luther King, Jr., and Barbara Harris.

These are all lives filled with the unexpected possibilities of God. They said yes when others wanted them to say no. We too, like Mary, can magnify the Lord with our lives, for it doth not yet appear what we shall be . . . for eyes have not seen, ears have not heard, neither has it entered our hearts the things which God has prepared for them that love God!

E.R.A.

G. DANIEL JONES

Text: Luke 10:38-42

Introduction

The Equal Rights Amendment failed to be ratified. This nation apparently was not ready to endorse such legislation, which was thought to be femininely inspired, too radical, and too revolutionary. The gospel reveals much to us about Jesus' relationships to women. He accepted women to be among his closest followers. In the Gospel of John there are seven episodes recorded of Jesus' encounter with females, namely: the miracle of Cana (chapter 2); the meeting with the Samaritan woman at the well (chapter 4); the apprehension of the adulterous woman (chapter 8); the death of Lazarus (chapter 11); the foot anointing before the Passover (chapter 12); the crucifixion (chapter 19); and the resurrection encounter in the garden (chapter 20).

There is no aspect of human life with which Jesus is not concerned. He is concerned about children, men, women. He is concerned about the religious and the nonreligious. The young, the aged, the sick, the handicapped, the poor, the rich, the enslaved, and the disenfranchised are concerns of our Lord. He is in the business of releasing captives. Temple-member Jews and Gentiles were both concerns of Jesus. Let's focus on his concern for women as shown in his relationship with Martha and Mary.

According to author Wilma Scott Heide, if a feminist is a person

---

G. Daniel Jones is Senior Pastor at Grace Baptist Church, in Germantown, Pennsylvania. He received the 1984 American Baptist Ministers Council sermon award for E.R.A. advocacy.

who respects the rights of every individual, whether male or female, then Jesus must have been a feminist.

In addition to the sexism faced by all women, black women must also contend with the problems of racism and poverty.

Economically, the differentiation between black women and middle-class Anglo-Saxon women is in distribution and access. This was pointed out by Elaine R. Jones, Esq., Deputy Director of the NAACP's Legal Defense Fund, in a speech to the female members of the National Bar Association. Wherein white women in many instances have privileges of entry but are often faced with an unequal distribution, black women are not only deprived of an equal distribution, but because of racism are often denied access, or entry, especially in traditionally male-populated areas of competitive advancement. However, distribution and entry, as concerns, affect women universally. While many white women who have gained access to the ball or to the grand reception are concerned about the size of the slice of pie, respect from the host or hostess, respect as a thinking person from the escort, image as either person or ornament, black women seldom have access to the party, proper garments, transportation to the affair, or adequate child care service at home. Even if able to attend the reception, they are often greeted by their same-sexed white counterparts with severe questions as to access.

For example, the 1984 Democratic candidate for Vice President of the United States had access, while distribution of votes and power were real concerns. Currently, the woman who sits on the Supreme Court bench has access. Her minority status highlights the problems of sexism and distribution. Black women and other minority women have neither the luxury of access nor equal distribution. Granted, this is an exaggeration, but the point is that racism is a barrier even among same-sexed individuals. However, the issue of ERA affects all. The Declaration of Independence as it was originally authored did not include blacks in its pursuit of liberty. Blacks at that time were not considered people. How can one be entitled to rights if he or she is not a person? Later, through centuries of the civil rights movement, all people were recognized. Following the passage of the Fifteenth Amendment to the U.S. Constitution, the women's movement began. It was fostered by some because now illiterate black men had a privilege to vote. "Whiteness" was thought to be superior. Those thought to be inferiors must never have rights that superiors do not have. This was the beginning of the women's movement in the early part of the twentieth century. Even though African Americans as a people were not the primary or secondary focus in the women's movement, there is still some universal good.

Interculturally and interracially, the concerns of liberation for women are similar, but the agendas differ, largely due to racism. Equal pay for equal work is universally good. Federally subsidized day care is universally good for society. It reduces extensive welfare payments and expenditures, which enables single welfare parents to support their families with dignity. The right to choose one's future or destiny is universally good. Legal protection against domestic violence and rape is good. Affirmative action in training programs and empowerment is good. This will reduce controversial handouts and dehumanizing programs. More reputable representation of females in the media is good, rather than having them presented merely as sex symbols. Entry into traditionally male-dominated structures of the world of work is good.

Since Christ liberates and sets captives free, since Christ is the Savior, since Christ is no respecter of persons, the church must be fully involved in human rights, civil rights, children's rights, women's rights, and people's rights. The rights of the poor, the deprived, the suppressed, the oppressed are all concerns of Jesus. Jesus is concerned about the least.

Jesus was a friend to Mary and Martha. He was a family friend. On a given day he visited the home of Martha and Mary. Martha's choice or values included house duties, domestic chores, extending gracious hospitality, volunteer servanthood, and acceptance in a role given by family and society. She was rigid and inflexible. Mary's preference was listening to Jesus' teachings. This was a break from Jewish tradition and traditionalism. The men were expected to be taught in rabbinal studies. This private audience changed the world, and challenged sexism as being unacceptable to Christ.

Mary had access, took advantage of it, and received ample distribution because of her aggressiveness, coupled with the grace of our Lord. Martha, the "uptight" sister, could have had greater access, and could have received a satisfying distribution. It was Martha who initially invited Jesus to her home. She chose to distance herself, and she also chose to hinder her sister from having her needs met through both access and distribution. Ironically, considering Mary's total access, she never offered or encouraged her sister Martha. Nor did she defend her own position. Jesus spoke for her; she was silent enough to allow the spirit of Christ to speak. She was militant enough to let her actions speak.

ERA: Equal Rights Available

Martha had the same access as her sister Mary. Mary profited from the presence of her Divine Resource. Christ was present. Christ is ever present. The Word Mary bountifully received became real. Christ Jesus entered her home and her heart.

Martha chose to complain about her sister. Her sibling rivalry was clearly apparent. Even today a competitive spirit seems to be the norm. Perhaps Martha resented the courage of her sister's striving to become free. Martha saw Mary move to a higher level. No doubt because of Martha's own insecurity with regard to her femininity, personhood, self-esteem, and value system, she avoided confronting Mary directly, and instead asked Jesus to reprimand Mary for refusing to assist her. In confidence, Mary chose to sit at the Master's feet.

ERA: Empowered, Reassured, Affirmed

Martha was enslaved to traditionalism. She was enslaved to a locked-in system of society's expectations. Mentally, she was happily imprisoned.

When we break from enslaving traditionalism, Christ gives us power.

Empowered to be courageous in choosing the higher;
Empowered to grow by caring;
Empowered to be privately tutored by Jesus the Master Teacher;
Empowered to be unintimidated, unshaken;
Empowered to stand, sit, or run if it pleases our God.

Christ gives each of us the power and right to have human dignity, to be respected and treated as a person, and to be protected against discrimination without regard to age, sex, race, class, marital status, income, national origin, legal status, culture, or condition in society. Christ frees us if we would but fall at his feet, hear his Word, and allow ourselves to be empowered by him, as we develop into whole persons.

Mary was affirmed by Jesus. The fact that Jesus felt that Mary was okay was a positive affirmation. Worship is in order. Study is in order. The practical application follows divine instruction and a divine encounter. Even though Martha may have been attempting to raise herself up by putting Mary down, Jesus picked Mary up to the highest of levels by affirming her through approving her faith and course of action. Jesus affirmed Mary by stroking her in the presence of her verbal attacker and abuser. Jesus affirms all of God's children as having worth. ERA—Jesus empowers, reassures, and affirms.

Mary was reassured by Jesus' interest in her as an individual. He had come to her home. He gave her an audience. He shared himself with her through one-to-one interaction and communication. She could see God in Christ. She found joy in his presence. Because of the dialogue between Mary and the Son of God, she understood herself better, and she understood him better. Possibly her self-esteem rose. Her reassurance confirmed what it is to begin with the basics. "Seek ye first the Kingdom of heaven, and all else shall be added." "Wherever Jesus is 'tis heaven there." In spite of Martha's interruptions, frustration, and controlling attitude, Jesus had patience with her. He also reassured her as he demonstrated his love. Because he is the Lord, the Spirit of the Living God, he ministered to Mary as well as Martha. *Empowered, Reassured* and *Affirmed.*

ERA: Eternal Riches Awarded

Mary chose freedom and salvation. She chose liberation and salvation. Salvation makes possible good works. Due to the choice, good works may be expected. Eternal riches? *Eternal Riches Awarded.* No one can take the wealth away from someone who has received directly from Jesus. "Mary has chosen the better part," said Jesus. The inference is, Why not decide now to choose me over anything or anyone else? "If I am lifted up, I will draw all humankind unto me; for I am a part of you and you are a part of me."

This is the last verse of this passage. The older folk once told us to study, learn, embody the truth, and acquire knowledge. Once we acquire it, no one can take it away from us. When one dwells in Christ, the *Eternal Riches Awarded* can never be taken away. The one who is awarded has wealth to share. *Eternal Riches Awarded* include: atonement, grace, propitiation, forgiveness, justification, and no condemnation in those who believe. They further include: imputation, adoption, sanctification, redemption, glorification. *Eternal Riches Awarded.*

The eternal wealth includes salvation. We are saved from guilt and the penalty of sin; saved from the power of domination and sin; saved from the present enslavement of sin and liberated into the presence of God. *Eternal Riches Awarded.* Mary has chosen the good part.

Many women in our local church have been qualified for leadership positions but they have been overlooked in favor of some man, Brother X, simply because he was a man. Is that right? The women were qualified and knew the work. Women have supported and boosted men in secular employment, but when promotions were granted, they were overlooked simply because they were women. Is Christ pleased with that?

In the church community, we are threatened. In traditionalism there is always a degree of comfort or complacency. Christ shook traditionalism, when it was practiced simply for the sake of tradition. The ancient Jewish temple-goers also were traditional by being addicted to the Law, while attempting to follow in "robot" fashion. Was the Law written upon their hearts? We, too, are threatened on our boards, commissions, and committees even in our own churches. We are threatened by female ecclesiasticism, by the increased entry of females into the gospel ministry, and by diaconate appointments, followed by ordination. That threatens us. We must seriously consider what is the will of God. We will be punished by God unless we go to God in earnest prayer, realizing that God is no respecter of persons. A man is not superior simply based upon his anatomy. God created male humans and female humans, both in the image of God.

One man within our church fellowship was disturbed about a matter. A very competent woman was teaching one of our midweek Bible sessions. This brother refrained from attending class because a woman was the instructor. What a shock to discover that *his God was that small!* I would not worship a god who was so very small. God calls to ministry those whom God desires to call. In fact each Christian is called to ministry. If it is God's will, even the rocks may be called upon to cry out and give God praise. I believe that any kind of human-inflicted abuse, oppression, suppression, or domination is against the will of God. To the one who lets go and lets God, *Eternal Riches* are *Awarded.*

Conclusion

There is equality in Christ. "There is neither Jew nor Greek, there is neither slave nor free, there is neither male nor female" (Galatians 3:28). There is wholeness in Christ. There is completeness in him. This equality in Christ means mutual respect, mutual partnership, and equal opportunity. It means that one sex has no superiority over the other. It means promoting human kindness and human interests by eradicating any form of oppression, slavery, or suppression. It means that sexual hierarchy or pecking order for advancement is a no-no. It is a no-no in the kingdom of God. It means that a change is taking place; a change must take place, for Christ's sake and for the sake of righteousness. It means that Jesus is change. He is the necessary change. He is the light. He is hope in a world of social darkness.

He calls us, male and female. He calls us from all walks of life. He calls us to awaken from centuries of spiritual slumber. He calls us to risk. He calls us to launch into the deep.

The New Testament is God's second half of God's own written revelation, God's housecleaning tool, God's amendment; God's restructuring device, God's printed historical search for humankind.

When the news was revealed about Jesus' resurrection, the disciples did not have a monopoly on receiving the news first. The women were the ones to run to spread the Good News that "He is risen." God needed strong men. God needed strong women. God needed them to work together as partners in ministry. God still needs the co-ed population worshiping, working, and witnessing.

Mary chose the good part which shall not be taken away from her. What about our church? What about you? Amen.

A CALL TO WITNESS

LEONTINE T. KELLY

TEXT: Isaiah 43:1-10

Would you think of a definition of "saint"? My two favorites are: the one by a little boy who says a saint is someone that the sun shines through; and the one I am more comfortable with because it fits more of us, especially me, is that a saint is a sinner who has tried.

Let's look at the word of the Lord in the Book of Isaiah 43:1-10. The tenth verse reads: " 'You are my witnesses,' says the Lord, 'and my servant whom I have chosen, that you may know and believe me and understand that I am He. Before me no god was formed, nor shall there be any after me.' " Coming from earthquake country, I find that when terra firma moves the sovereignty of God is very clear.

In Jesus' ministry, when he and his disciples were come together, they asked him, " 'Lord, will you at this time restore the kingdom of Israel?' He said to them, 'It is not for you to know times or seasons which the Father has put in his own authority. But you shall receive power when the Holy Spirit has come upon you; and you shall be my witnesses in Jerusalem and in all Judea and Samaria and to the ends of the earth' " (Acts 1:6-8).

As the prophet Isaiah speaks the word of restoration and hope to a people in captivity, we are called to witness to a sovereign who calls us by name. I found myself going back to the Scripture again recently. I happened to be at Wesley Seminary in Washington, D.C. When I finished my lecture in the chapel, a young seminarian came forth to thank me for prophetic words and then said, "We are going

Leontine T. Kelly is Bishop, United Methodist Church, Retired, and Visiting Professor of Preaching at Pacific School of Religion, Berkeley.

to ask the bishop to pray for us and lift us because San Francisco has been hit by a severe earthquake." I had to admit that at that moment I was more "mama" than bishop, for I had a twenty-three-year-old daughter who lives with me in the San Francisco Bay area. I did pray, and it was with a woman's heart, it was with a mother's heart, it was with a woman bishop's heart. It was with all that I am and who I am in the sight of God, for God has called me by name. I understand these words of Isaiah to a people, from a just and righteous God, who in vulnerability chooses the human creature to witness to the very character of God.

Listen to the words of a resurrected Jesus, the strongest witness of the Word itself in flesh, witnessing and defining witness in terms of specific ministry as he comes proclaiming the Kingdom of God. "The kingdom is here," Jesus says, and the possibility of modeling and living in that kind of power has already been given us.

There must be a difference in the way people read the Bible. I am convinced of that. I went to seminary so late in life that my children said, "Mama, you are going to be retired and ordained at the same conference." It almost happened, but not quite. There were all the miracles in between. And you have the sense of knowing that, as you read the Word, you're saying what may be considered the bottom up rather than what sees itself as the top down. It is a very clear message. I remember once going to San Francisco and, because I was historically the first black woman bishop in the kingdom in all denominations at that time, I was quite notorious. People were interviewing me everywhere and I remember a reporter who said to me, "Bishop Kelly, do you believe in liberation theology?" And I said, "You ask a black woman if she believes in liberation theology?" I have been trained in classical theology, but classical theology could not confront a Hitler, conformed too long to some idea of superiority of certain people. I learned as a girl why my own people, black people in slavery, accepted Christianity. I dared to ask my preacher father, "How in the world did our people buy the blond blue-eyed Jesus Christ, the only one in the Middle East? How did they buy God in this form even though they were being taunted by the persons who held them in bondage?" And I did find out, as I worked through Scripture and lived life, that the witnesses of God's compassion and caring and promise of faithfulness come to those who know that God is there. Nevertheless, the witness is forged in the midst of fire and that is why on Good Friday, black Christians knew who they were by the liberating message of Jesus Christ. They could sing, not "Were you there when they crucified *their* Lord?" but "Were you there when they crucified *my* Lord?"

Wherever the word of God goes around the world, it is heard and received in the heart of persons within the context of their own humanity, their own individuality, their own preconceived understanding that they are children of God. There is a freedom and a liberation that comes with that.

Being a woman is a joyous thing. I remember being called "Leon" so many times, once to the distress of an elderly man at a laymen's retreat in Virginia. When I walked in and he found out I was to be his roommate he said, "Oh, lady! You don't want to stay here with me. I've got asthma."

Sisters, there is an opportunity for a concerted effort of women of God to make clear the ability of the gospel of Jesus Christ to speak to the wholeness of all humanity. Wherever, whenever, the gospel of Jesus Christ is received, it becomes the liberating word of God. And persons empowered by the Holy Spirit to witness to this God are freely changed and are freed to be instruments to bring about change. It is the very purpose of witnessing. Most American women are not passive or submissive. We're not afraid to rock the boat or make waves. We are all called by the Holy Spirit, to witness, to make waves. Witnessing in the name of Jesus Christ is making a difference.

The gospel, when transposed from its biblical world to other cultural worlds, undergoes change itself, as well as causing these other worlds to change. The gospel is a very powerful thing. It not only changes human institutions and creates new values, but also changes the hearts of people. The wonderful thing about the gospel is that it could come in any shape and in any color. Furthermore, if it feels comfortable in a Western suit, it is equally comfortable in an Indian sari, or in a Japanese kimono. We have constantly underestimated the enormous changeability of the gospel of Jesus Christ. But it is this changeability that makes the gospel what it is, "the good news that God loves and saves people." God is God. God does not need our defense.

How can we serve this bold God with our timid faith? How can we follow this God whose frontiers are forever expanding, even when the frontiers of our theology are closed. It is this God who

changes, transposes, and becomes flesh in the human light. It is this
God who judges and redeems human beings and the world. As we
invoke the Holy Spirit to come to us, to recreate us, to make us new,
to use us as witnessing instruments of God's creative purposes in this
world, then we must expect bold transposition. The apostles thought
the kingdom of God would be actualized without a transposition of
the faith from Jerusalem to the rest of the world. They were happy
to be empowered by the Spirit to witness: they were empowered by
the Holy Spirit to preach, with power, the Good News of the Lord
Jesus Christ. But they wanted to confine their teaching and preaching
to the traditions and customs of the old world community even after
the Pentecost experience. They did not want to expand the gospel
with boldness to include membership in the community. It took a
Paul—oh, Paul never would have thought I would be here to say
this—it took a Paul to effect a change.

I remember the man who stopped me on my way to my church
one Sunday morning. He asked me, "Are you the woman who is the
pastor of the church up on the corner?" I said, "Yes!" He said, "You
are doing a great job." I said, "Thank you, you've made my day." I
started away. He said, "Wait a minute. Come back here. There's only
one thing wrong with that. You don't have any business doing it."
He began to quote my brother Paul, from Corinthians. Then I said,
"Sir, there are two hundred fifty children over at that church right
now and I don't have time to stand here and defend my ministry to
you. Besides, Paul didn't call me, Jesus called me." It took a Paul,
however, to interpret the grace of God to include the Gentile world.
Paul understood that the purpose for his salvation was not just to
accept the Word in the sight of God, but it was to push back the
perimeters of Judaism to understand the clear words of Jesus, "You
shall be my witnesses . . . ."

In a letter to the Romans, Paul reminds us that we are not called
to conform to this world but to become transformers by the power
of God's Spirit. Even Joel understood that new visions would be
needed and it would take the Spirit upon all flesh: ". . . and your sons
and your daughters shall prophesy, your old men shall dream dreams,
your young men shall see visions: And also upon the servants and
upon the handmaids . . . will I pour out my spirit" (Joel 2:28-29, KJV).

In this day as we witness earthquakes and hurricanes, we see
people, in the midst of these emergencies of the moment, forget

about who is who in terms of color or sex or class and begin to move together. These are earthshaking days, they are urgent days, and they are days in which the Spirit of God is alive in the world. But we close ourselves off and we must come in confession; we must be honest and call on God for mercy.

We have violated our faithfulness to God. We have not been God's clear witnesses of healing and wholeness for all nations and for all peoples. We dare to determine who is worthy of God's love and claim reward for goodness that is not evident in our society as a whole. Too few of us acknowledge God's sovereignty, too few live in obedient stewardship of God's world, too few care that we need God's mercy. We are timid people of faith. We have failed to confront with power the immorality of our society.

A quality of life, a wholeness of life, and an abundance of life are due every child of God at birth, not to be won as a reward, not to be begged for from other more resourceful nations, not to be proved worthy when human life is already worthy. I am reminded of a little boy who heard the creation story. The teacher told the story, "And God did this on this day and it was good, and God did this on this day and it was good." And the little boy finally said, "If it was all so good, what happened to it?" We have to admit *we* happened to it. And we continue to happen to what ought to be the wholeness, the *shalom* of God's world. The widening gap between the haves and the want-to-haves is appalling.

What do we *women* want? Don't take our pictures; we want the camera. Women, I call you to the totality of the global society of which you are a part. If the men will join you, do it; and if they will not join you, do it anyhow. Most people today are ill-fed, ill-housed and prey to preventable disease. More people today are undernourished, illiterate and living in urban slums than ten or twenty years ago. And racism is stronger now than it was when I was a child.

How do we read our Bibles? How do we study the word of God? What a challenge from a book that tells us to move out in boldness by the power of a God who will enable us to change the world. Listen to our language: "a permanent underclass." Should such a phrase be in the vocabulary of a democracy? Listen to the language we speak: "the feminization of poverty"—the very words we use seek to interpret the lives of women in terms like "homeless with children." The number of women who seek to rear families with very little is appalling, and the uncaring response of a government is more so. The church of Jesus Christ, it seems to me, is that place where as witnesses, male and female, we come together to dialogue, to hear one another's story, to be empowered by the Spirit, to move beyond, to go out into our world to make a change.

I can't retire. I have to keep going wherever I can say it is time for us to witness to Jesus Christ with power. You must model with one another what a Christian community of faith ought to be about. How are you going to accept women in churches who do not know that they are free, when you cannot accept one another even in the academic community? Who can define what God would call a person to do or be? Only God can do that. The Spirit moves as it will, through whom it will, whenever it will.

I wear a cross that was given to me by some of my Catholic sisters. I covenanted with them to wear this cross until they are ordained. Somebody asked me the other day, "Who do you plan to bequeath it to?" Their ordinations may not come in my lifetime, but no institution has the biblical right to determine who will witness for God. The written word does not tell us all that the women did, but we know the resurrected Lord spoke first to the women, and they spread the Good News. Our Lord has not ceased to speak to and through women, no matter how tradition and vested male interests may seek to limit the witness.

Joel's prophecy still holds, and women in this latter day do get the Spirit poured out on them, along with the men. The Spirit is moving today; it is moving here and now. All we need is to be open and understand that the foundations of our faith are not defined by the terra firma under our feet, or the buildings we build, or the material possessions we acquire, or our "success" models, even in ministry. The witness is that we are here to change the world, and the kingdom has already come, and we are the children of its Ruler.

God calls us; God moves us; God empowers us; God uses us as witnesses; and God goes with us. Ours is the privilege and the awesome obligation to preach the Word to all the world. Our strength comes from One who calls us by name, calling the people of God to *be* the people of God.

Women, that's your witness.

ADDITIONAL SERMON BOOKS FROM JUDSON PRESS

Best Black Sermons, William M. Philpot, editor. Sermons that emphasize black dignity and proclaim God's power. 0-8170-0533-1.

Outstanding Black Sermons, J. Alfred Smith, Sr., editor. 0-8170-0664-8.

Outstanding Black Sermons, Vol. 2, Walter B. Hoard, editor. 0-8170-0832-2.

Outstanding Black Sermons, Vol. 3, Milton E. Owens, Jr., editor. 0-8170-0973.

Sermons from the Black Pulpit, Samuel D. Proctor and William D. Watley. Thirteen sermons that call for a renewed commitment to discipleship. 0-8170-1034-3.

Sermons on Special Days: Preaching Through the Year in the Black Church, William D. Watley. Sixteen sermons for all celebrations of the Christian year. 0-8170-1089-0.

From Mess to Miracle and Other Sermons, William D. Watley. 0-8170-1154-4.

Those Preachin' Women, Ella Pearson Mitchell, editor. Fourteen sermons by black women that call Christians to develop positive attitudes and to find their identities by oneness in God. 0-8170-1073-4.

Those Preaching Women, Vol. 2—More Sermons by Black Women Preachers. Ella Pearson Mitchell, editor. 0-8170-1131-5.

Vision of Hope: Sermons for Community Outreach, Benjamin Greene, Jr., editor. 0-8170-1150-1.